DON'T WORRY, HE WON'T GET FAR ON FOOT

DON'T WORRY, HE WON'T GET

FAR ON FOOT

JOHN CALLAHAN

WILLIAM MORROW
An Imprint of HarperCollins*Publishers*

Grateful acknowledgment is made to the following:

"The Hanging Man," by Sylvia Plath. From *Ariel*, copyright © 1961, 1962, 1963, 1964, 1965, by Ted Hughes. Reprinted by permission of Harper & Row.

The following cartoons are printed courtesy of the publisher: "It hurts when I go like this" (page 170), copyright © 1988 by *Variations* magazine.

"First chance I've had to sit down all day" (page 171), copyright © 1988 by *Forum* magazine.

"Don't be a fool, Billy" (page 173), copyright © 1986 by *Penthouse* magazine.

"Efficiency expert" (page 175), copyright © 1987 by *Penthouse* magazine.

HarperCollins books may be purchased for educational, business, or sales promotional use. For information, please email the Special Markets Department at SPsales@harpercollins.com.

A hardcover edition of this book was published in 1989 by William Morrow, an imprint of HarperCollins Publishers.

FIRST WILLIAM MORROW PAPERBACK EDITION PUBLISHED 2018.

Designed by Diahann Sturge

The Library of Congress has catalogued a previous edition as follows:

    Callahan, John.
    Don't worry, he won't get far on foot / John Callahan.
      p. cm.
    Reprint. Originally published: New York: Morrow, 1989.
    ISBN 0-679-72824-4
    1. Callahan, John. 2. Quadriplegics—United States—Biography.
3. Cartoonists—United States—Biography. 4. Alcoholics—United
States—Biography. I. Title.
    [RC406.Q33C35 1990]
    362.4'3'092—dc20   89-40488
                                [B] CIP

ISBN 978-0-06-283696-0 (pbk.)

18 19 20 21 22 LSC 10 9 8 7 6 5 4 3 2 1

For my family and Debbie Levin

DON'T WORRY, HE WON'T GET FAR ON FOOT

CHAPTER 1

On the last day I walked, I woke up without a hangover. I was still loaded from the previous night.

It was 11:00 A.M., a hot July 22, 1972. I had no idea where I'd been the night before. Past experience told me I had an hour or so of grace before withdrawal symptoms set in. So I was a man of leisure. First thing: light a cigarette. Everybody in the house was gone. I'd slept right through the taped mariachi music that Jesus Alvarado turned on at 5:30 every morning to pump himself up for another day of house-painting. Music from a Taco Bell in hell.

Alone, I could pad down the hall to the bathroom in the nude. I took a piss, making the sign of the cross in the toilet with the stream of urine, a compulsion I hated but couldn't shake. Then I flushed and hopped into the shower.

Even there I had to smoke, holding the butt above the curtain with my left hand while I scrubbed the left side of my body with my right, then switching it over to my right hand so that I could use my left to scrub my right side. It takes imagination to support a three-pack-a-day habit.

Shaving, I checked myself out in the mirror. A big, six-foot, three-inch twenty-one-year-old Irishman, body hardened by work, ruggedly handsome if you discounted a little acne scarring, flaming red hair. Not bad. No handicap with the girls and a nice contrast to the creative artist, poet, and songwriter hidden somewhere within. But I felt the edge of nervousness. After all, what was I doing getting out of bed at almost noon? I was supposed to be job hunting, down here in Buena Park, California.

Drying off, I began to feel hungry, a sign that pangs of withdrawal were imminent. Stepping down the hall to the kitchen I dug a tortilla out of the fridge. No point in waiting for the oven. I just singed it on the stove element and spread on some peanut butter. Nutrition had no priority. The key thing was to get to the liquor store before the paranoia cranked up. I was beginning to feel very nervous just thinking about it.

So I went back to the bedroom and put on thongs and jeans and the Hawaiian shirt I had bought, which the Alvarado family had snickered at when I moved down here from The Dalles, Oregon, a month or so ago. The full heat of a Los Angeles summer day was leaking through Mrs. Alvarado's spotless venetian blinds. I lit another cigarette. Outside, the Alvarado Doberman growled briefly at some passerby. In the L.A. suburbs attack dogs and eight-foot-high chain-link fences seemed to be standard household equipment.

Nearly noon. My nerves were telling me: get to the liquor store. I set out on the six-block hike, irritated at myself for not being able to enjoy the beauty of this day and the beauty of my life in general. The sky was brownish blue. The street seemed unnaturally wide and the palms that lined both sides of it had a grimy tinge. The white adobe-style tract houses, all with yucca plants, were pleasing enough to my eye, but I could sense the occupants peering out at me through closed blinds. The air was stifling. I felt certain the sky was going to cave in before I could get a drink.

Without breaking stride, for there was no time to waste, I tried to light a cigarette but burned my fingers instead. The shakes! My heart was starting to pound. I had to do something about it. All these staring people I couldn't see knew all about me, my blackest secrets, my entire history: that I was a depraved alcoholic, the worst that ever lived. Two blocks to go.

The booze—I couldn't let myself think about it. I took deep breaths. I tried to concentrate on something. I made myself stop and pet a cat. I prayed, "Jesus, let me make it to the store!" My hands were clammy, I was starting to sweat and my mouth was totally dry. I was so scared. What if I lost control, flipped out and started to scream? Each thought was worse than the one before it. I just kept forcing them back down again. Why did I have to be this way?

The store was at a major intersection. Whatsa-Vista Ave. and Three Millionth Street stretched away in that uncompromising L.A. perspective that implies, if not infinity, then at least the curvature of the earth. Uncounted liquor stores, Jack-In-The-Boxes, 7-Elevens, topless bars and rent-to-own furniture marts serviced hundreds of characterless "towns" just like Buena Park. A faint smog hung over everything, an atmosphere of boredom and menace.

I bought a half-pint of tequila and stayed to chat a while with the owners, just to show how in-control I was. In fact they would have to have been blind men not to notice that my hands were shaking when I handed them the money. They probably knew my whole story. They could tell how ashamed I was. So what? Liquor store clerks are probably sworn to silence, like priests.

Next door there was a topless bar, the Club Heaven. Sometimes I stopped in there for an eye-opener, but the dancers were floppy-breasted and middle-aged, and there were more hookers than clients.

Maybe I could get all the way back to the Alvarados' without opening the half-pint and taking an embarrassing first hit in public. Besides, as I headed back down the block, my hands were shaking too violently to open the bottle. I'd drop it on the sidewalk. The neat little half-pint, so inconspicuous and sophisticated, was snug in my hip pocket.

One of the whores in front of the Club Heaven yelled after me, "Hey Whitey, wanna date?" A lowrider cruised slowly by, full of tough-looking kids. Mexican gangs shooting from cars supposedly killed somebody nearly every day and had shot a three-year-old girl not far from the Alvarados' the week I moved in. She had wandered in front of a shotgun aimed at somebody else.

In the heat the air seemed to have no oxygen. This featureless city, a thousand suburbs stitched together, stretched out around me. I felt unconnected to any of it. I had traveled maybe half a block before I stopped, willed my hands to be fairly still, and twisted off the screwtop. I took a big hit and jammed the bottle back out of sight as fast as I could, hoping nobody had noticed. If only I could shoot the stuff into my arm and not have to wait for the booze to take effect. I was panicked that the stuff wouldn't start to work on me before I went nuts. What had I gotten into? How could I be so scared?

But seconds later I didn't have a problem. I could feel the warmth coming through my body. The noise was turning down in my mind. The faces were pulling away from all the windows. Walking back to the house, I did not feel quite normal yet, but the edge was off. I was hoping to get back quickly so I could take a second shot. Then I'd be steady enough to light a cigarette.

At the house the sound of a ghetto blaster playing "White Bird" by the hippie uplift group It's a Beautiful Day announced that Teresa "Terri" Alvarado was back for lunch. I didn't like Terri. The Alvarados' teenage daughter was a self-confident little number who probably thought I was a bum mooching off the household, when in fact I was paying room and board and helping her father, Jesus, rebuild his boat.

I went into the bathroom and filled a glass with water. I pulled my hooch, took a snort, then took a little shot of water and another great big hit of tequila. Now I was feeling good enough to go out front and say hello to Terri and a cutey-pie Anglo friend of hers, who looked up at me with a big smile and said, "Hi. Hear you're from Oregon. How you doing?" But I didn't try to hit on her. It was time to hop into my Volkswagen and set out on the job hunt. Business first.

It was really hard being alone down here. Maybe a little detour to the beach would cheer me up. I felt guilty about driving while loaded but any second the Mexicans might whip around the corner and blow me out of the driver's seat with a Gatling gun. I had to keep a little glow going.

I liked the idea of half-pints because I wouldn't get stoned too fast, but this one was almost empty. So I stopped for a beer at a bar in Costa Mesa, where nobody really spoke any English, as it turned out. In fact, I recognized this bar. Jesus Alvarado had taken me there before, during one of our shark-fishing expeditions. Once a week he took a day off, we went out on a charter boat, and while a bunch of old men tried to catch sharks, I climbed up top and got drunk with the captain.

I loved lazily drifting on the California sea beneath the expensive mansion-strewn cliffs of Malibu. On the deck below me Alvarado's pals got tangled up in about four million dollars' worth of shark-fishing equipment. Their hats were full of hooks. I used to wonder why they didn't just throw the hats into the water.

I finished the drive to the beach. The half-pint was gone but I bought another at a Payless Drug, stuck it in my jeans, and wandered out onto the sand to watch the people: hardbody girls in bikinis, guys straight out of soft-drink ads jogging with their dogs, fat old women with Scotch coolers full of picnic.

A girl in a bikini stopped for a chat. I fantasized she'd take me back to her bungalow, we'd have sophisticated L.A. sex, I'd move in, her love would turn me into a normal person forever. Then I froze up: She must smell the booze on my breath. She must know.

Alone again, I thought about how I got here. I came down to L.A. with Jesus' brother Rico, a drinking buddy up in The Dalles. Rico was a minor pool hustler and a major ladies' man, using the Bible as his main instrument. Not that he could read it. He had simply memorized some key passages. But Rico divined that the

Anyone could see I was in trouble and I resented having it pointed out.

Word of God had a calming effect on women. So he became a born-again dyslexic.

He decided that we should go visit his brother and family, who were on vacation at Lake Havasu, Arizona. Then we would go on to L.A. His license had been revoked for drunken driving, and I'd lost mine too, but it somehow fell to me to drive Rico's ancient Triumph sports car while he preached nonstop.

"Remember what the Lord said, Johnny . . ."

"Don't give me the Lord bullshit, Rico."

At virtually every gas station Rico leaped out to try his scriptural wiles on the local talent. Fortunately he was such a glaring, transparent phony (he even had a crucifix tattooed on his right hand) that few fell for his cornball. Otherwise we might never have reached L.A.

"Have you heard about Jesus Christ?"

"Get the fuck out of here, Spic!" And we were back on the highway.

We drove down 101 through the redwoods. I remember how magnificent they were and I remember thinking, God, I wish I could enjoy this sober. Then we crossed the mountains and drove down through the Nevada desert, through Las Vegas, where we did not gamble but drank; and across Death Valley with the top down, where we did not perish of thirst, to Lake Havasu, where London Bridge, imported by a gang of insane developers, shimmered improbably in the 110-degree heat. It looked like the set for a Mad Max movie. Jesus, a relentless boater, ran his outboard nonstop on the lake. The rest of us just stayed up to our chins in it, the only way to survive.

I hit it off with Jesus, so it was decided that I would live with the family for a few months while Rico wandered back up to Oregon to spread the Good News. I thought, I'm going to be really proud; a small-town guy moves to the big city and makes it. So far so good. Only a month in town and already I was drunk on the beach at lunchtime.

I got back in the VW. I bought a six-pack and got a little cardboard sandwich from a Jack-In-The-Box. I drove back along straight, broad, anonymous streets through the car lots, liquor stores, antique shoppes and lube-job places of Bellflower, Anaheim, Orange, Buena Park. Home after Home Sweet Home for the employees of McDonnell Douglas, Hughes, Lockheed, Northrup, and other southern California defense industries where, in 1972, business was great.

It must have been 3:00 or 4:00 P.M. when I got back to the Alvarados', because Jesus was home. He was chatting out in the driveway with a man in a blue pantsuit sitting in an electric wheelchair. I thought, God, now I'm going to have to meet this guy. I'd noticed him around a lot. Jesus spotted me hurrying across the lawn. "Hey, Callahan, come over and meet Bill!"

My small-town experience was limited concerning disabled people. When I was a preschooler a man stopped in the courtyard of the apartment complex where we lived and sat under a willow tree. He played spoons on his wooden legs until our parents hustled us away from him.

Bill was paunchy and red-faced. I felt nervous and slightly hostile, thinking, Why does he have to wear a leisure suit? I shook hands, and Jesus said, "Look at this!"

Jesus handed me the guy's ballpoint. It was a special pen. If you held it up to the light and rotated the end like a kaleidoscope, you saw a 3-D picture of a guy with an enormous hard-on getting a blow job from two pretty girls. Laughing, I offered them each a beer from my six-pack. I hoped Jesus wouldn't ask me if I'd found a job.

Inside the house Terri and Mrs. Alvarado, a withdrawn woman who had to put up with me because I was pals with her husband but tried hard to ignore my very existence, were at work on dinner. Terri invited me to come along to a party with some of her friends. As an Oregonian, I was a little put off by these L.A. parties. Nobody knew anybody else and nobody seemed to care. Everyone had a tan, was an entrepreneur, and talked incessantly about the state of his colon. Terri must have needed a ride. She was being extra nice, so I said, "Sounds great."

To keep my nerves calm, I had a couple of belts in my room. After dinner Terri's friends came, we wedged into my Volkswagen, introduced ourselves in a minimal way, and drove across Orange County to Anaheim.

The party seemed to consist of twenty or thirty people gathered around the pool, all talking about the latest boutique drug. But some of the women were topless, which pleased me greatly. The odors of hamburgers and chorizos on the kettle cooker mingled with perfume, chlorine, and marijuana in the early evening heat.

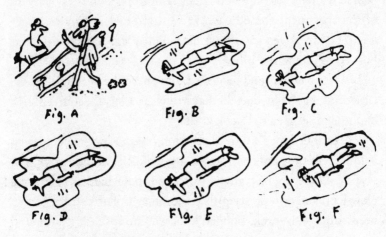

As I got older my drinking followed a fairly predictable pattern.

I met a blonde of about my age, and we hit it off. Things were looking up. But right in the middle of the conversation I got nervous and excused myself to go up to the bathroom. Sitting in the can, I fished out my bottle and dumped a shot into my beer—a tequila boilermaker. I checked out my beginner's freckle tan in the mirror and calmed down.

Returning to poolside, I found that the girl had left with some of her friends. Her biographical tape—marriages, divorces, lovers, therapy, diet—had begun to bore me anyway. "I've just gotten off meat and now I'm kicking dairy products." What did she eat? Saddle burrs? Somewhere down at the other end of the pool I could hear Terri's precocious drawl. "Jeezzuss, maann. Far fuckin' ooouuuttt."

Then I was buttonholed by a fellow who struck me as an obnoxious pest. He was very aggressive. Dexter was the sort who tries really hard to be liked, but ends up being detested because he's a blowhard. I've always attracted weirdos.

The sun was going down and the party was no longer much fun. He said he knew of a party with better "babes"—"It's great! You'll love it!" With my used VW and his connections, anything seemed possible, even the half-hour drive to Long Beach. We couldn't find any host or hostess to thank, forgot about Terri and her pals, just split.

We made a full ten blocks before pausing at the first bar.

Several ten-block units and bars later Dexter, who was driving at the time, leaned out and puked all over the side of my car. I made him stop at the next gas station and wash the barf off with a hose from the pump island.

He felt up to stopping at the next bar so I could replenish my stock of tequila and latch on to another six-pack for boilermakers. We had a drink while the bartender was getting it together.

Eventually we drove on in the general direction of Long Beach, passing en route the famous Knott's Berry Farm. Neither of us had ever been to Knott's Berry Farm. So we decided to stop and sneak over the wall and enjoy all the rides, the Wild West stuff and the famous berries free. After a lot of effort we got over the wall and stumbled along the brick paths from amusement to amusement.

Then we spent another twenty minutes crawling back out over the wall again, even though no one would have cared if we'd just exited through the main gate.

It was dark now. I was doing the driving while Dexter explained why he was the Cunnilingus King of Orange County. "I just *love* yodeling into it!" he slurred. Still, he was company, and it was kind of fun to be with a guy my own age for a change, having a few laughs.

By the time we hit another topless bar I was almost too drunk to get out of the car. Dexter swore this place was special, the dancers were great, etc., so I made the effort. I remember falling asleep with my head on the table, my cigarette burning me awake. I was starting to doze off again when Dexter began pounding me on the back and shaking me violently. "Callahan! Look! She took it all off! She's bottomless! Wake up!" I opened my eyes to a double vision of blurred muff.

The parking attendant tried to stop us from getting back into the VW. "You guys are in no condition to drive a tricycle!" Dexter took the wheel. He's too drunk, I thought fuzzily. He's way too drunk. . . .

I can remember leaning my head against the window, feeling all cozy and safe. It was the state I'd been aiming for all day, a sense of being in a warm womb.

Then, a gentle confusion. Red lights. Shouting. Something about a blowtorch and a gas tank. A cacophony of faraway sounds and lights.

Dexter had mistaken a Con Edison pole for an exit and had run straight into it at ninety miles an hour. The Volkswagen had folded up like an accordion, causing minor injuries to Dexter but neatly severing my spine. I didn't notice, though. I was too drunk.

CHAPTER 2

I was born directly into the Church at Saint Vincent's Hospital in Portland, Oregon on the fifth of February, 1951. The way with illegitimate Catholic babies in those days was to remove them from the mother at birth, presumably to prevent any bonding, put them in the care of the nuns for six months in case the natural mother should change her mind, and then give them up for adoption to some devout couple.

Thus on the eleventh of July I was handed over to David Callahan, a grain broker, and his wife, Rosemary, who thought themselves unable to have children of their own. They were mistaken.

My adoptive mother became pregnant the following December with the first of five natural Callahan children, three boys and two girls.

While I was still in diapers the Callahans were transferred eighty miles up the Columbia River to The Dalles, a small town that they hated. To a Portlander this was exile. Never mind that the place was deeply rooted in history—the greatest rendezvous of pre-Columbian America, where thousands of Indians gathered annually to net the abundant salmon, trade, gamble and tell lies. Never mind that the landscape was of surpassing grandeur. In 1954 The Dalles was a sleepy wheat port with a small Irish Catholic community surrounded by snakes, lizards and Mormons. The nuns who taught in the parochial school left no doubt which was worse. Whenever a busload of Mormon kids went by on their way to a picnic or a ball game the sisters would hiss, "You know that they're going to Hell on that bus, don't you?"

My earliest preschool memories were of the church itself, built in the 1800s to serve the increasing number of shepherds who had come over from County Cork. The soil of the Columbia River Basin was prepared for grain by millions of sharp hooves. The sheep were mostly gone but the Rileys, the Kennedys, the Learys, the Sullivans remained. During the long masses, whenever I was not kneeling, jumping up, standing, sitting, kneeling, jumping up again, never imagining that I was an aerobics pioneer, I liked to study the farmers dressed in badly cut pinstripe suits like dead men's clothing, their thick necks topped by homemade haircuts, their hoarse, pessimistic voices intoning the Latin hymns.

The building itself seemed magnificent (it has since been designated an historical monument). The wainscoting, the lectern and the screens were of polished oak, finely worked, and the stained glass had been brought from Germany. The altar, altar rail and tabernacle were gold, the ceilings frescoed with the lives of the saints, the plaster walls above the wainscoting covered with icons between the stations of the cross. A choir of nuns lifted their voices at the back.

Into this splendor filed an amazing collection of rubes and yokels. I especially remember one old man with a flowing white mustache, in an old suit, arm in arm with his old wife who, due to a stroke, could barely walk. I was sure they had been born senile.

Bringing up the rear were the Daltons, always late though they had probably gotten up early on their remote farm, in ancient suits, hand-me-downs and faded dresses. The whole family looked like Hoss Cartwright, even the women. Boone Dalton, one of the youngest, would be in my first-grade class. They sat up front and bobbed their soup-bowl haircuts one by one as they genuflected and shuffled sideways into the pew. I thought they lived in a state of mortal sin from tardiness.

The Callahans also sat near the front, with mother and father on either end of the squirming line of kids. I was never bored in church. I was always being popped by my dad: "Don't stare! Look ahead at the altar!" No use, I was straining for every morsel of interest and excitement. I always secretly wished Father Flynn would one day announce to the congregation, "And now, let us join together for a few moments in staring openly at the Daltons for a good laugh." Instead, he was droning the *introit ad altare dei* and old Pete, who acted as if he was senile *and* had Parkinson's, was voicing the responses about ten minutes late, often in the middle of the succeeding passage. Pete also limped and so it was he who was charged with passing the collection basket.

My father always fell asleep during the sermon. He was a big, highly visible man, about six foot four and two-hundred-plus pounds. His neck craned back and to the right over his shoulder; with his mouth gaping straight up at the ceiling frescos, he would begin to snore. No one ever woke him up. He would rouse himself just before the snores crescendoed and shout, "God, my neck is killing me!" Then he'd remember where he was.

Often we'd go to Portland for the weekend and attend mass at huge Saint Madelaine's Church, Grandpa Otto's parish church. Grandpa Otto habitually turned his hearing aid off for the duration of the mass. When the Sign of Peace came in after Vatican II, the priest would announce, "You may offer one another the Sign of Peace." You were supposed to turn to your neighbors left and right, offer your hand and say, "Peace be with you." So I turned to Grandpa Otto and said, "Peace be with you, Grandpa Otto! Peace be with you, Grandpa Otto!"

And he yelled back, "Huh? What? Whaddaya want?!!" Every man, woman and child was staring at us. Even the saints were rotating on their pedestals.

Of course I have some regular preschool memories as well: playing along the creek with my friend Jimmy Riley and falling in four or five times a day, exasperating my mother because I was always wet and muddy from the pursuit of frogs; building log rafts that would have floated if the creek had been more than six inches deep; sleeping out in homemade tents; being tucked in at night warm and secure in the basement room I shared with Kip, prayers heard ("God bless Mommy and Daddy and Kippy and Tommy and Murphy and Terry and Ritchie and the dog and . . .") and kisses given. Even at that age I was drawing pictures for my mother, who understood me better than anyone.

My parents made no bones about my being adopted and revealed it to me very early on. They'd heard of a case where the parents waited until their son was grown up, and when they told him, he went crazy. On the other hand, I was the only kid in the family with bright red hair and ultra-pale freckly skin. To save endless explanations Dad would tell people that I took after his redheaded Grandma Ethel, who had come over from Ireland. I always felt funny about that.

My brother Kip, who was nearest to me in age, had black hair. Tom, who was four years younger than me, had our mother's light brown hair and could more plausibly have been my sibling. My sisters, soft-spoken Murphy with her piercing blue eyes and rowdy, fun-loving Terry, both had jet-black tresses. Only Ritchie, born when I was twelve, had even slightly reddish hair, and by then it was too late. Where had he been when I needed him? I had to change his diapers, which I loathed and which I still guilt-trip him about (in front of his fiancée).

The Callahan kids were tall, good-looking, and witty. There was always a joke going in that house. In spite of the usual kid brutality—Kip and I rode Tom unmercifully, and everybody ganged up on Murphy because she was so shy and gentle—I have good memories of my preschool and gradeschool years.

Yet I'm convinced that I experienced a sense of loss even as an infant, and as childhood wore on, I spent more and more time by myself, thinking about my own strangeness. I didn't feel I belonged and I felt guilty that I felt that way. I often wondered about my birth parents. Was my mother a queen? A whore? Could I locate her and surprise her, say, at a bank teller's window? "Yes, I'd like to cash this check, MOM!"

These feelings gave me a big chip on my shoulder toward my adoptive family, which led to trouble during my teenage years.

I had an early fascination with death, of which there was plenty. When I was eight, Grandpa Joe skidded off the icy road into the river while bringing a load of Christmas bicycles up the Columbia Gorge to us from Portland. I insisted on going to the funeral, though the rest of the family thought I was nuts. His death, I think, was a harkening back to my real mother, who was lost to me at the time as if she were in the land of the dead.

They held the Rosary in a funeral home chapel in northwest Portland, just across the street from the window in which I am writing this. I can remember the women filing by to kiss his waxen and unnatural forehead. I was aghast that people would kiss his dead body as it lay in the casket. On the other hand I didn't blink for minutes because I didn't want to miss seeing him twitch. It never entered my eight-year-old head that he *wouldn't* twitch. It was all fascinating: the weeping, the guilty undertakers, the dismal organ music, all of it enveloped in a deep floral pungency.

The day was dark, and rainwater gleamed on the steps of Saint Madelaine's. There seemed to be hundreds of people listening to the eulogy, which went on for an hour. Then came the long procession in glistening black Cadillacs, winding up the hill to Calgary Cemetery above town, with motorcycle cops weaving in and out to stop everybody else at the crossings, which made me feel very important indeed. The family sat under a tent at the graveside with easy chairs for the older women and folding chairs for the rest of the family. More weeping, while the rain puddled up on the tarp provided by the undertaker to cover the fresh dirt.

I enjoyed it all.

Home was a three-bedroom house on Dry Hollow Road across from a vast field of weeds where we hunted lizards. The blue-bellied kind were okay. The yellow-bellied kind could kill you. Our basement was finished to accommodate more kid bedrooms and the decor was churchy: plug-in picture of Christ flashing His illuminated heart in the hall, holy-water dips under each light switch, so that if you were electrocuted it would be in a state of grace. There was a library equipped, oddly, with a set of the Russian classics. In adolescence this would be my territorial niche. Insomniac, I spent the nights in the library reading, writing poetry, drawing, thinking, being alone. Eventually I started sleeping there as well. I delighted in staying up all night working on my latest creation to dazzle family and friends. My family was always in awe of my artistic talent, and Mom and Dad were especially supportive and encouraging.

Sleeping in the library also helped me to avoid my dog. The whole family except me hated pets, but I had finally talked my father into what looked at first like a small Lab. He quickly grew into a fat brute exactly like a black pig, and he had none of the sweet nature the breed is known for. He insisted on sleeping across my legs, cutting off my circulation; if I tried to move he attacked me, biting through the covers into my legs. When we finally got him off the bed he moved to the back-door landing, halfway up the stairs between basement and kitchen. If I tried to sneak up the stairs he would nearly kill me. I thought of the saint who was plagued by a satanic lion roaring at the foot of his bed. The dog's undoing came when, with advancing age, he decided to get surly with grown-ups instead of just us kids. "Boy, when they start that nippin' business . . . ," said Dad as he prodded the swinish brute into the station wagon for a "ride in the country." My only other attempt at pets was a guinea pig that died even before I finished paying for him. I buried him behind the garage but kept exhuming him to see how his decomposition was progressing.

During World War II my father had fought in the Papua, New Guinea campaign, a corporal in a regiment of army engineers specially trained for amphibious assaults. The unit made over sixty landings and two-thirds of the men had become casualties by the end of the war. He would never talk about it; but I think he bore the scars. He was extremely short-tempered, apt to fly into violent rages. I'm sorry to say that as I grew up, I learned just how to provoke him and often did. His approach to parenting was to try to control everything. Even when we were little, mealtimes were like dining with a drill instructor.

"Sit up straight. Keep quiet. Get your elbows off the table. Watch your milk, you're going to spill your milk. Don't talk so much. Talk more. Eat your vegetables. Move along." He stood by the table with a butter knife held by the blade, ready to thwack any errant elbow. There was a rod on top of the refrigerator for major offenses. He was relentless in tracking you down if you tried to get away with something. I imagined myself after several succeeding lifetimes somewhere in India, where a stranger approaches me and says, "*You* broke that basement window, *didn't you?*"

Friday night after a meal of "fishdicks" (who would have thought that fish had dicks?), we were made clean for confession by a shower and one of Dad's haircuts.

"A gentleman gets his hair cut every week," he was always telling us. He was absolutely obsessed with short hair. Armed with electric clippers and a jar of Butcher's Wax, he created flattops so short that the sides of our heads were shaved white and with stubble so stiff I feared I would slash open my pillowcase. "How can you *stand* to have that hair touching your ears?" he would ask in wonder. Visually, what he left was a little half-inch picket fence, with maybe a sixteenth of an inch left on top where the bumps on my head surfaced like a volcano out of a flat lake. I always thought it would be more expedient to have our ears surgically removed. Then he would send us up to show mother, who pronounced our cuts "masterfully done" and "sharp-looking." Thirty years later she admitted to me that she really thought they were appalling.

In third or fourth grade I had to start wearing glasses, which, added to the flattop, made me look like the Ultimate Drip. My self-esteem was totaled, and when the Beatles came along, it got worse. I can remember sitting in the classroom eating my lunch sandwich, with my deskmate, Suzie Ballinger, laughing uncontrollably at the sight of my nude temple muscles grinding away.

Saturday nights we went to confession, bored to tears and weary from standing in the line that moved slowly backward to the confessional booth, always facing the altar. I imagined an express lane ending at a special booth with the sign "Eight Items or Less." Every twelve feet or so was a pillar against which we could lean for a moment's relief. Meanwhile our minds were occupied making up sins. You had to have a lot or you might end up confessing a real one. There in the booth, with the forbidding silhouette of the priest behind the silk screen, it was better to have stolen some cookies. Then, all you heard in the surprisingly human voice was, "Are you sorry for your sins? Say a good act of contrition and seven million Hail Marys."

We didn't dare skimp on them, but ripped through the prayers as fast as possible so the others wouldn't suspect we were real sinners. If I had admitted my real sins, such as masturbation, I was sure the priest would have ripped open the screen, climbed through and said, "Look, you little son of a bitch, nobody's ever done anything *that* bad before. I'm going to kill you right here on the spot and embarrass you in front of the whole church!"

I would have sooner confessed to murder. After years of going to confession with Father Flynn, I'd theoretically stolen the entire Grandma's cookie factory.

When I was six, school began amid so much pants wetting the nuns had to wear tennis shoes. Jimmy Riley's corduroys flew from the top of the jungle gym like a sodden flag while he cowered bareass in the Sister Superior's office, missing recess. It was a time we would devote to catching lizards to put down girls' dresses.

At Saint Mary's Academy, grades were divided one through four in one classroom, five through eight in the other across the central hallway, with a small gym and an office on the end. That's all there was to it, yet my memory tells me we were always in line. "Silence in line." "No talking in line." We went in line to assembly, to recess, to confession, to class, to the toilet. I often wondered what happened to the old nuns when they retired and had no more lines behind them. I am sure that if the children had ever mutinied, they would have run away in line.

The nuns, Sisters of the Holy Name, took no guff. They were highly trained, excellent teachers. No one got "passed along"—you were held back if you didn't perform. Even in the early grades there were two or three hours of homework every night. Emphasis was on the basics: math, English, penmanship and, with a grade of its own equal to the others, deportment. I did well and more than once classmates asked me to tutor them.

The nuns were all-powerful. They could crack you across the knuckles with a ruler or make you stand in a wastebasket. On one occasion Tom Quinn, who was incorrigible, had to eat soap. He liked it, which really pissed off the nun. Once Jimmy Riley was caught doing something so horrible that he was spanked by *two* nuns—Sister Sergeant Bilko and Sister Butch Johnson. To underscore the theme of discipline, we were not allowed to dress like normal children. We went all over town in uniforms that set us self-consciously apart: salt-and-pepper cords, blue long-sleeved sweaters over white shirts, black brogues.

The first Friday of every month was a "holy day of obligation." Our parents dropped us off at church, which was clear downtown, at 6:30 A.M. High Mass lasted until about eight. Then we all climbed up the hill to the school, two miles away—in line, of course. Then and only then could we open our lunchboxes. We'd eaten nothing since the previous night because we were fasting for communion and, self-conscious about eating in public, the most I could manage at that point were a few furtive nibbles. Spirituality is all very well, I thought, but I'm just a kid. I didn't want to be a saint, just a cartoonist or a CPA.

A nun's or priest's birthday was a feast day, a school holiday. If the janitor had a birthday, it seemed, we were out of school. The result was that our school year ended about the Fourth of July.

Holy cards were the prize money of Saint Mary's Academy. Often having worked your butt off to win the spelling bee or the book-report contest, you soon caught on that you were not going to get a trip to Disneyland or a blender. Instead you got a holy card of Saint Michael or Saint Teresa. When I first heard of holy cards I thought, I didn't know the saints played baseball. These consisted of pictures of the saints, usually down on one knee with glowing halo, and a light coming from a cloud into their faces, which wore expressions of what I can only describe as X-rated ecstasy.

Sister Joseph of Mary was a huge nun, quite masculine in appearance, with great beetling eyebrows, like Ernest Borgnine in drag. She was so large we used to joke that the vast wooden cross at her waist was the True Cross. Like all the nuns she had no pockets but tied things to her girdle with string instead. She could reach down and haul a big pair of scissors up like a fish from the depths of her hem. Sometimes, standing next to her, I would get lost in the many black folds of her habit.

Sister Joseph of Mary's emotional needs were evidently not satisfied by her role as a Bride of Christ. She was a frustrated mom, and I was unlucky enough to be chosen her surrogate child. I probably got the part because I was a straight-A student, and was installed by her as fourth-grade class president. She kept telling me I was special; I reminded her of Ratty in *The Wind in the Willows*. She insisted I write special essays, and once I was obliged to write one comparing and contrasting myself with the imaginary rodent. She did her best to cut me off from the rest of the kids—I could not play at recess but had to sit beside her on a bench. "You're so much more *special* than those other kids," she would whisper. "Why don't you try to make Toby X and Mark Y feel better about themselves?" One was grossly overweight and the other abysmally stupid. I can imagine myself sitting on that bench and thinking, Boy, this will be called child molestation twenty years from now. I was held up as a good example. One day she noticed that I looked a little pouty and depressed and announced that nobody was going out to recess until the class made John Callahan smile. Needless to say I wouldn't. I was damned if I was going to smile. So we missed recess, and I was damn near hung from the school shrine.

I really felt at the time that this woman was being cruel to me. I drew a caricature of Sister Joseph of Mary, grossly naked except for her headdress, with stretch marks all over her stomach added skillfully with a red pen, and passed it around. Inevitably Sister Joseph of Mary saw the ripple of laughter. She took the paper away and instantly saw that it was the work of the talented and diplomatic John Callahan. My days as a surrogate child came to an abrupt end.

Sister Joseph of Mary was crushed and betrayed, as only an ugly person who has given love can feel crushed and betrayed. In later years she resigned her vows and became a radical lesbian, but then she worked hard to reinforce the feeling that I was personally responsible for the Agony of Christ. At least.

I had no reason to doubt that this was true. I was at the age where I literally ran upstairs because I had been told that the Devil was waiting to catch me by the heels. At the same time, though, I got satisfaction out of finally having pissed off Sister Joseph of Mary enough to get her off my back. I was readmitted to lizard-catching society.

Then there was the matter of being an altar boy. This was not optional. Either you made it to the Altar Boy Picnic or you were considered to be a fag from Hell.

This meant wearing cassocks so short that everybody could see my pale shins and hours of memorizing unintelligible Latin under the red nose of Monsignor McCarty, who would have tested .066 blood alcohol.

"Ah, ah, *adeumque pontificat avem tutem mea . . .*"

"No, no! *litificat*," you little idiot.

He was often so drunk during mass that he swayed his way along the communion rail, slapping the host on the tongues of the faithful with trembling fingers. I followed along holding a golden pallet under the communicants' chins to catch any crumbs of the sacred wafer that might fall and amused myself by seeing how close I could come to their Adam's apples.

In spite of such low comedy, we lived in a state of pious fear in which Satan could have his way with any boy who didn't do his math assignment. In my family, anyway, Death and Judgment were always at hand. We spent the weekends visiting dying grandparents in nursing homes in Portland. Although The Dalles was surrounded by great hunting and fishing country and was a camper's paradise, my father was not interested in such things; though once he did take us to a "pay 'n' fish" pond—we didn't get a bite.

Instead, he and my brothers were obsessed by team sports. Hours and hours were spent practicing; even more time was spent in front of the tube. I tended to tune out when the jargon started. Sacks and slam-dunks held no interest for me. Ironically I was the best athlete in the house, a pitcher with a natural screwball while still in grade school. I played on the all-star team and was carried off the field when I struck out the final batter to win the big game. The family doctor once spent hours trying to convince me to aim for the major leagues. But, perhaps in resistance to my dad, I dropped sports before high school, even though that would have been *the* route to popularity.

I craved popularity because I knew myself to be a black sheep, a total stranger in my own home, fearful and neurotic. I hid in the basement when we had guests. I felt guilt over my lack of family feeling, guilt over the insomnia that kept me awake in the library reading Turgenev and Tolstoy and Chekhov when everybody else was sleeping, guilt over the artistic impulse that made me a loner, writing or drawing for long hours. Just before high school, things were compounded by a case of virulent acne. It was so bad my classmates played Connect the Dots on my face.

When I was thirteen and on the verge of high school, I discovered that there was a medicine for my guilt, if not for my acne scars. At my grandmother's wake I pilfered some gin from a table laden with booze. I loved it, and drank until I passed out. I threw up violently in the middle of the night, of course, but that didn't matter.

In 1965 I graduated from Saint Mary's and began public high school. After the standards I was used to, it was boring and so easy that I mostly didn't attend. My buddies and I spent our days drinking in whatever house was free of parents. When we were licensed to drive, we bought "beaters" and tooled around, swinging past the school where girls were lolling on the knoll to expose their underwear to passing citizens, driving up to a bluff to get stoned on the cheap grass that was becoming plentiful and drinking some more.

Our clique included Aronsen, a 140-pound, six-foot-six albino with totally white hair. His mom owned a beauty parlor and was never at home, so that was our party house. Then there were Swartzburg, who was crazy and carried a gun; Burns, who loved to taunt Aronsen; Wells, whom we called Bullnuts; Meyers, also crazy; and mild-mannered Foley, my best friend.

Foley and I were famous hunters, having begun shooting birds with BB guns, then gone on to "below the waist" wars in which we stalked and shot one another, but only below the waist. Unless we got really angry. We then graduated to .22 single-shot rifles and started in on ground squirrels, of which there are millions in The Dalles. We got bored with playing Attack of the Ground Squirrels and with knocking magpies out of apple trees and soon decided to go deer hunting. Once, stoned on pot, we actually drew down on what we thought was a deer and put about a dozen .22 long-rifle slugs into it before we realized we had just slaughtered a nice Angus cow. We had to get part-time jobs to pay back the enraged farmer.

We went to all sorts of trouble to get to Portland, eighty miles away, to score drugs. In those days you went to a certain park, offered a ten-dollar bill, and either had it stolen or exchanged for half a Baggie of the strongest pot in the universe. It was like LSD. Typically we drove around with the windows rolled up in order not to lose any of the precious smoke. Cops were always stopping us for one reason or another but never seemed to notice the cloud of fumes that billowed out when we rolled down the window. I always imagined the cop would then drive to a head shop and buy a Janis Joplin poster for reasons he never understood.

We'd gather in Aronsen's living room, which was entirely decorated with fine antiques. Aronsen was constantly worrying about us bumping into something and breaking it. He always had his eye on us lest we sneak back into his mother's bedroom, where she kept her liquor, and steal more than we'd already stolen that day.

I remember one scene where Burns, who was extraordinarily hairy—Aronsen used to put him on mailing lists for women's depilatories—was taunting Aronsen. "I'm not going to be able to let you ride in my car anymore, Aronsen. You're frightening away the chicks."

Aronsen muttered, "Right." He was playing with a Zippo lighter, tilting it so that the flame caught the open lid.

"I don't know . . . they call you 'The Worm.' Did you know that?"

"That so?"

"You've got to get a tan. Think of your nonexistent sex life, why don't you?"

"I know, I should. You're right."

"Besides, it's good for the old self-esteem."

And Aronsen kept playing with the lighter, which was getting hotter and hotter. I began to have a sense of impending doom about Burns, who was going on and on. Usually Aronsen was not so cool, and I can remember being thrown up against the lockers at school for drawing pictures of him nude with a tiny weenie painstakingly detailed in red pen.

By now Aronsen was smiling and saying, "Yeah, Burns. Sure, Burns. You're right, Burns."

Finally Burns said, "One more thing . . . ," but he never finished.

Aronsen flew across the room, grabbed Burns out of the antique settee, threw him down on the Persian carpet like a polar bear straddling a bald chicken. Then he ripped Burns's shirt open and branded him on the chest with the white-hot lighter.

We were horrified and delighted to see such a show. The scar turned out to be in the shape of a fish. It was appropriate in the end, since Burns has recently become a Born-Again Christian.

Foley's father had just bought a drive-in movie theater high on the windy cliffs of The Dalles, where Indians used to dry their fishing nets. He was spending a fortune to fix it up. The screen had been routinely blown down and the place looked beat to hell. We hung around the snack bar in the middle and played grab-ass with the girls. Foley and I would work the ticket office and then join the rest, stoned on cough syrup and sneaked-in beer. When things got dull, we did the Ball Walk. Six or seven of us would expose our scrotums, choking them out through our zippers with our penises tucked out of sight. Then we would line up single file and, with heels together, toes splayed out and pelvises thrust forward, would waddle through the snack bar like obscene penguins. The disgust on the faces of the shrieking girls racing for the exits was delightful.

It was at this stage of my emotional development that I fell in love for the first time. Paula Sobaczech was parked in the front row with Foley's sister Jean one night, and Burns and I just kind of sauntered over. After a while we slipped into the backseat, the better to make conversation. After a further while, Burns got into the front seat with Jean, and Paula came back to me.

A hot summer wind rattled the old movie screen and raised whitecaps on the once-wild waters of the Columbia below, now ponded behind The Dalles hydroelectric dam. When the show was over Jean drove her big pink Chrysler, a gift from her dad, aimlessly around the country roads through orchards and wheat fields. Below, the river shimmered in the summer moon, while in the backseat Paula and I kissed and gazed. In the clear heat of those summer nights the girls wore halters and shorts, while we boys went bare-chested. I felt a tremendous, giddy excitement.

Above all, I was flattered, for Paula was one of the cutest girls in school, a fresh, blue-eyed brunette with a nut-brown tan and delicious curves.

At the back of my mind, I was thinking, This midnight romance is all very well; but in the light of day she'll see things differently. She'll see how fucked up I really am.

But in the clear light of the following morning, Paula, in crisp white short-shorts and a white blouse knotted beneath her breasts, was eager for a long, slow, hand-holding stroll in the woods above town. It was the start of a long summer of country walks, of aimless drives in my windowless '58 Chevy beater, of envious sarcasm from my buddies, none of whom had a girl remotely as good-looking as Paula. They'd drive by and hoot, "There's Callahan with his girlfriend—he's finally fallen!"

I was a late bloomer. Even at eighteen, part of me would have felt more comfortable pulling a girl's pigtails or putting a frog down her blouse. But, Paula! Once she put her hand lightly on my thigh, and I almost drove the Chevy off the cliff. I would have been trying to unbutton her blouse on the way down.

Paula was a good Catholic girl. Passionate kissing was okay, but she allowed no hands on her opulent breasts. So getting her bra off became the main obsession of my life. My brain seethed with deviousness and planning. Perhaps my hand would brush against one of those milky-white love balloons, casually and in passing. A short time later the same accident would happen, but with just a hint of suggestiveness. And again, still very casually, but now definitely erotic . . . and so on, until she noticed what I was up to and slapped the piss out of me.

A couple of times I got her blouse open, and once I even got her bra off. Since she was very uncomfortable about this, the victory probably had more to do with her devotion than with my seductive skills.

But in spite of repeated proofs of her affection through the summer and fall, and into the following winter (once we walked through the old graveyard in a rainstorm), I didn't ever really believe Paula loved me. On the basis of absolutely no evidence, I always felt that I was somehow forcing myself on her. She couldn't *really* want me to walk her to school. She wasn't *really* glad to see me when we ran into each other in the halls. She didn't *really* want to be seen with me in front of her friends.

In fact, what Paula didn't like—really—was me drunk. And that was how I was handling my insecurity about myself and about her: I spent almost my entire senior year of high school in the bag. I would show up at Paula's house barely able to drive and badger her until she got into the car. "Callahan, you're so impulsive . . ." She must have been terrified, because several times I drove into things while she was with me. On one occasion I drank half a fifth of 150-proof rum, skipping class to do it, picked Paula up and took her to my parents' house, where she sat and made polite conversation as if she didn't notice the almost falling-down state I was in.

In spite of scenes like this, she remained willing to sit up on top of the cliff in the windowless Chevy and snuggle with me while the midnight winter wind howled around us.

I began to drive a stake between us. Although I became frantically jealous at the slightest hint that she was flirting with another boy, I decided that I didn't really like Paula. Paula Sobaczech, I decided, was really unattractive and bitchy (the strongest thing she ever said to me was, "You'll never marry, Callahan."). I saw her less and less and finally cut her out of my life completely.

I locked myself away in my basement bedroom and sunk into a black depression. My buddy Joe had access to homemade rotgut plum wine his father made, and I always had a gallon of the awful stuff around. I lived down there with the wine and my guitar for weeks, playing Dylan's "Just Like a Woman" over and over, alternately despising Paula (I'd show her, by becoming rich and famous) and yearning hopelessly for her.

This was my first engineered breakup with a woman, my first confused attempt to get back at my birth mother for abandoning me. There would be many others; but now I stayed away from any involvement with women for two years.

Instead I concentrated on staying stoned, my main concern, and on raising hell. As campaign manager to student-body presidential candidate (and drinking buddy) Sam Dick, I was the author of the stadium-length "Erect Dick" sign done in hard-to-erase sideline chalk. That rated a three-day suspension. Even more important was that I met a kindred spirit who became my best friend until his death.

One day a friend we called "Nevada Smith" came up and said, "Callahan, I'd like you to meet Kurt Crawford." We extended hands, grasped palms, and Crawford pulled my hand down nearly to his crotch. I fell down with laughter. Everybody in those days was homophobic. Who *was* this guy? In spite of his Saxon name, he had that Irish light of humor in his eyes.

Kurt and I became good old drinkin' buddies. He was charismatic and very handsome. He was a real ladies' man. Kurt always had to have a relationship going; whereas I was just going out with girls. We dated together, drank together, took LSD together. For me acid was not such a hot idea. In fact, I bummed out entirely. My friends drove me home and I could barely open the door, since there seemed to be about two hundred doors. My mom found me cowering in my bedroom in the pitch-black dark consumed by visions of paranoid guilt. A doctor had to be called to bring me down with a giant shot of Thorazine.

My father, who could be driven into apoplexy by the ordinary behavior of small boys, now found himself confronted with an over-six-foot-tall drughead and drunk, who came home, often as not, raging with anger. Actually, I had been out of his control ever since the day, at age twelve, when I hit one of my younger brothers in the butt with a baseball during one of our regular sibling fights. The blow was nonlethal but it hurt, and Kip went crying to Dad. Dad came storming down the basement stairs, and I ran away. I got as far as the woodpile before being brought to bay. I picked up a Pres-to-Log and threw it at him, then another and another. I couldn't believe it; I was actually fending him off. Then I ran into the bathroom and locked the door. Since it was a basement bathroom, the window was small and high, and I couldn't crawl out of it. I heard him screaming, "I'm going to get an ax and chop the door down!" Fortunately my mother was able to restrain him.

Often my alienation from my dad—I hated his guts from age eleven on—extended itself to the whole family. Not long before the Pres-to-Log incident there had been some disturbance at the dinner table and Tommy, who at age six was some five years younger than me, screamed, "You're not even one of us!" I burst into tears. I really did feel the pain; but also I was trying to milk the situation and get my dad to beat the living shit out of my brother, which he did, of course. Whenever he punished one of my siblings instead of me, I had a *guilt-free* excuse to condemn him.

By the end of high school my relations with my father were chillier still. It was high time to move out; but when it came time to pick a college, I froze solid. Either it would be as dull and repressive as school or, worse, it would require serious work, thus interfering with my life as a knee-walking drunk. So, Kurt and I took jobs as orderlies at the local state mental hospital. My first home away from home was a room in the nuthouse-staff dormitory. This was a spacious Georgian brick building up on a hill behind the nuthouse, with black tile floors that were always being scrubbed and large rooms that came complete with maid service. We spent our time there drinking, playing guitar and sneaking in girls.

When an apartment became a social necessity, we took the first of a whole series of apartments together. For me, Kurt was the perfect companion. We'd drive up to a Dairy Queen together and he'd say, "Okay, Callahan, let's go in and scream our orders." I didn't take this seriously, but Kurt walked up to the young girl at the counter and did just that, scaring her silly. In any restaurant his first act was to excuse himself, go to the men's room, and emerge trailing a long tail of toilet paper, which he seemed not to notice. His mind was always active, just like mine. Two mental escape artists—and we needed to be.

As "Mr. Callahan, Psychiatric Aide #1"—that's what it said on my badge—I got to supervise ninety retarded men on one ward. Take them to the bathroom and dodge their pee. Give "Vernon" 800 milligrams of Thorazine in his eggnog and try to spot his psychosis coming back before he had a chance to kick some janitor in the nuts. In which case it was off to electroshock again.

There, with Kurt and four other psych aides, I got to assist elderly Dr. Wacker in the performance of his chief duty as director, which was to slam enough volts to fry a steak through the noggin of any patient who gave the least sign of becoming a problem. Kurt and I held the shoulders of the patient, Jim and Chuck held the hips, and Jack held the knees—I forget who had the feet. And Dr. Wacker applied the electrodes to the temples with his badly-chewed fingernails. Each time permanently erasing a large hunk of personality and memory. If anybody was in that nuthouse via an incorrect diagnosis, it wasn't incorrect for long. Before the treatment the patients got a shot of some muscle relaxant that reduced a screaming maniac to a docile cadaver with a loose, flapping tongue and bugged eyes. The whole body would jump into the air and spasm violently like a shark does after its head is exploded by one of those shotgun sticks. Two or three sessions with old Dr. Wacker and these patients were ready for a lifetime as institutional zombies. Deep inside, I felt awful pity for these poor slobs.

I slammed the lid of my mind firmly down on these emotions. Dr. Wacker himself drank heavily at each day's end, I noticed. He was a balding closet queen who wore a special pair of prosthetic shoes to conceal (unsuccessfully) the fact that his left leg was shorter than the right, and who preserved his respectability with a "white" marriage to a (presumably) frigid Nordic blonde we all yearned to thaw. But she was off-limits. Instead Kurt and I picked up two hitchhikers, who moved in with us for a while. One of them screwed Kurt and the other tried to screw the still-virgin

Callahan, when we were sober enough. That was convenient, except that one day we were skinny-dipping, drunk, in the cold Columbia and somebody stole all of our clothes—and our towels. The girls took this commonplace prank badly and got even madder when Kurt and I insisted on driving home, slowly, through the busy downtown business district. They moved out.

Then, early that fall, I met Cathy, a friend of Kurt's. She was auburn-haired and wore autumn colors, and her body, thinner than Paula's but just as delicious, exuded a sweet, smoky perfume. Best of all, she wore boots. She seemed more understated and at the same time more sensuous than any girl I'd known. She fell so completely in love with me that it was obvious even to me, the uncontested self-doubt champion of The Dalles.

Cathy lost no time getting rid of my virginity. Within a few hours of our meeting we were alone in my bedroom and she was very gently undoing my shirt buttons and belt buckle, lowering me down onto the bed and in general taking the lead in a nice way. Being naked under the covers with her was so exciting that I thought my heart was going to blow through my chest, but that was just openers. Though I had no basis for comparison at the time, it so happened that we were ideal lovers for each other. Every move was effortless, every response synchronized as if by magic. We seemed to flow into each other like the confluence of two rivers.

Afterward I felt very grateful and warm toward her, and we were a couple. But, unlike Cathy, I didn't fall in love, a fact I concealed from her but that, paradoxically, may have been one reason for the lack of nervous tension, the ease I felt when I was with her.

My drinking continued unabated and so did the surreal quality my life took on while I was working at the nuthouse. At this time Kurt and I lived at the top of a huge old four-story Victorian boardinghouse and we had a very stupid, large, and strange-looking dog whose legs were so short he could have been a cross between a Newfoundland and a boa constrictor. One day we were sitting around smoking pot and drinking beer and playing fetch with a tennis ball. The dog would chase, bring it back, then we had to pry it out of his lips so that we could throw it and he would chase it and bring it back again. Finally Kurt banked the ball off the wall, and we watched it bounce across the room. It bounced and bounced, clear across the room, with the dog jumping after it, and finally went out the window, as did the dog. It was his last jump and his best.

When we raced downstairs, he turned out to be not quite dead. Hoping no one had seen anything we hustled him off to the vet for a merciful injection.

We were rapidly turning into mental patients ourselves. We came to work drunk in order to bear the sight of the ninety retarded loonies weaving around and going through their unique cycles of repetitive gestures. We stole patient uniforms, slippers and all, and careened through downtown, flapping and twitching until the cops picked us up. We used to steal pills intended for the patients so that we would be as stoned as they were. We were nineteen, and the sight of the wards full of contorting, gyrating bodies making noises like Halloween had shaken up our reality systems, such as they were.

I remember a patient named Timmy, the product of incest. He was a very pretty and effeminate twenty-four-year-old male. Totally, 100 percent retarded, he was capable only of walking around hallucinating twenty-four hours a day. Sometimes I would study him. He walked around with his little hands out like the pope giving benediction and with an almost orgasmic ecstasy on his face. Other times he had a look of total horror as if he'd seen

Dr. Ruth, Betty Friedan, and Mother Teresa all at once. Nobody ever got his attention, except perhaps the homosexual patients, who were always trying to lead him away into a bedroom.

A patient named Gary flapped his hands inanely whenever he became excited. He could work himself up into some state that was almost masturbatory, with a crazed, blissful grin as he flapped harder and harder, to the point of damaging his hands. We were there to keep him calm, but sometimes I found myself unable to resist getting him started.

"Guess what were having for dinner, Gary?" (Flap. Flap.)

"Hot dogs!" (Flap, flap, flap!)

"And that's not all!" (Flap! Flap flap flap flap!)

"There's *chocolate pudding* for dessert!" (Flap! Flap! Flap-flapflapflapflapflapflapflap!!)

One day, just as Gary was ready to fall over from flapping (he had already begun to pee in his pants), Nurse Phillips happened by and instantly sized up the situation. I was summarily dismissed, booted out of the nuthouse. Nurse Phillips probably saved my sanity when she canned my ass.

Kurt and I lived together a little longer. We had both bought big motorcycles, a 750cc Norton for me and a big racing Triumph for him. Real death machines. I can remember riding in the rain, stoned and drunk at 120 miles an hour, in perfect rhythm and grace on twisting two-lane black-top roads. On mescaline the road just felt like chocolate syrup.

Cathy had become more and more attached to me and had gone along on all our drinking bouts, never protesting. But now that I was out of work and seeing more of her, my attitude toward her began to sour. Every evening we made love in my bed, but it got to the point where I didn't even bother to walk her home. It finally dawned on her that things were not right. One day she said, "You know, you're just using me. I don't think you really love me. Is that true, John?" And when she saw the guilt on my face, she picked up her coat and walked out the door.

I was crushed. Once again I was abandoned—never mind that I'd asked for it. I went into a depression deeper than any I'd known before or have known since. I became a prisoner in my own apartment. At first I paced around and drank; later I just sat on the bed and rocked myself in the fetal position, going out only for booze. It was the dead of winter, and for hours I'd just sit there next to the oil heater and tremble. I couldn't joke or smile, even with Kurt. My whole spirit felt raw and bruised. I planned my suicide, knew just which cliff I'd drive off—when I could work up the energy.

Eventually I went back to my parents' house and tried to explain what was happening. My mother decided that what I needed was to get busy and sent me out to weed in the garden. After a while she saw me sitting beside the beds: I was too depressed even to pull weeds. Next she sent me to a clinic downtown. The indifferent doctor gave me Thorazine, and I walked around like something out of a George Romero movie, with my mouth hanging open.

For weeks I ate my meals at my parents', not that the atmosphere was tolerable, but just to have someplace to go each day. That was a technique to keep some residual sanity; so was going to the bathroom for a sip of water, an alternative to a leap out the window.

It was my father who found me the way out. He got me a job with his friend Bob Wilson, a wheat-and-cattle rancher. Suddenly I found myself miles away, in a place that looked like the landscape of the moon, working with people who snickered at the mention of "depression"—they worked far too hard to get depressed.

On the Wilson ranch, everybody was up at 5:30 for a lesbian-sized breakfast of home-grown bacon and eggs. By 6:00 A.M. I'd be out on some godforsaken patch of prairie, digging postholes all by my lonesome. In to lunch we'd come at noon, and then it was back to the rockpile until well after dark. We were supposed to knock off at 5:00 or 6:00 P.M., but nobody ever quit much before 10:00.

At first I remained insomniac, lying awake in my basement bunk—just like home!—filled with depressive pain. But a few days of the Wilson regime had me dropping in my tracks the moment I got close enough to the bed for it to break my fall. So much for *angst*.

Since this was a ranch, I figured that on Saturday night we hands would mosey on into town, have a few drinks, shoot up the saloon, and generally kick back. But in the real world of the Wilson spread, there was always an emergency, and nobody ever got to town. So during my months on the ranch I didn't drink either.

A typical ranch disaster marked the end of my tenure out there in the wide-open spaces. A whole bunch of cattle died of bloat when some yo-yo put too much salt in their feed. The carcasses had to be disposed of before they ripened in the early-summer heat. It fell to me to attach each bloated corpse to an antique four-wheel-drive pickup and haul it up a steep track to the lip of a canyon, into which I then dumped the animal's remains for later burning.

Just once—but it was enough—I forgot to switch into four-wheel before climbing the hill. Halfway up, the ancient truck stalled and rolled back onto the towed cow, its wheels off the ground. The carcass burst in a gush of incredible odor, summoning flies from three neighboring states.

My parents' neighbor was head foreman at the huge Martin

Marietta Aluminum plant, an infernal region nearly as big as the town itself. Under the Old Pals Act, I was hired as a "extraman"—a summer replacement—at an astounding ten dollars an hour, top industrial wages for those days.

The plant and everything in it was on an inhuman scale, dictated by the aluminum-smelting process. A central corridor as wide as a freeway ran for half a mile under an eight-story-high tin roof. At right angles to this corridor were five pairs of "rooms"— vast bays each containing forty smelting pots the size of a large yacht and roughly the same shape. Forklifts the size of army tanks roared around carrying huge vessels—"cruisers"—full of the molten aluminum. Everywhere snaked electrical cables as thick as elephants' trunks, tended casually by ex-navy electricians.

The smelting of aluminum requires such extreme heat that it can only be generated electrically, which is why the plant was in The Dalles, right next to a hydroelectric dam. The four hundred smelting pots in the plant were in effect gigantic electrical resistors with enough juice to lay Don King's hair back down again.

As an extraman I was expected to do any job in the plant after it was explained to me once, even though a mistake on my part could easily have killed me or another worker. In retrospect it seems astounding that they would let a nineteen-year-old kid into the driver's seat of a giant rotating forklift carrying tons of molten metal, much less expect him to pour it, without spilling, into the trays where it cooled into ingots.

But in the ultra-macho atmosphere of the plant, sink-or-swim was the rule. I punched in each day with Mike Bishop, another summer kid. We had slightly long hair under our hardhats, the source of much merriment as we walked the gauntlet of rednecks and sheepfuckers who had worked this job for twenty or thirty years. To them we were a couple of queers.

We worked rotating shifts: seven days of day shift, followed by a forty-eight-hour break; then seven days of swing shift, followed by one and a half days off; and finally seven days of graveyard. I remember exhaustedly sitting at the edge of the plant watching the sun rise. We were then given a four-day "weekend," after which the whole thing repeated. The heat was appalling. If I got a moment to step outside and drench my entire body, boots and clothes with a firehose, thirty seconds of raking sludge from the surface of a pot would dry me right down to the skin again. Just once I showed up ten or fifteen minutes late. The head foreman putted up on his Cushman scooter. "Johnny, your dad is my best friend," he told me, "but if you do that again, you're outta here."

I wasn't. Mike left, along with the other extramen, at the end of the summer to attend college; but I stayed on for two years. The hard work, the weird hours, the exhaustion and the demonic heat made it impossible for my depression to catch up to me, even though I drank as hard as ever on the weekends. I was proud to be able to hack it, to earn the respect of the old-timers and to acquire a nickname—"Professor," of course. I was also laying by thousands of dollars, enough to start college when I chose, get married and start a family—or drive to L.A. in Rico Alvarado's sports car and spend the next six months drinking.

For the moment, though, and thanks to my father's intervention, I was making it.

Not Kurt, though. He had discovered paint. This was so odious to me that I began to be alienated from him. He would spray the same kind of canned paint graffiti vandals use into a plastic bag, cover his face with it and take huge, hyperventilating breaths until he was in another world. Where he went, even Timothy Leary would have been loath to follow. He became more and more self-destructive as time went on. He began to abuse his girlfriend. He became isolated. No matter how hard I drank, I could never catch up with him.

Riding along the main street on his Triumph one day he slowed down for what he thought was a double trailer rig pulling out of the alley in front of him. When he figured to clear the second part of the huge truck, he twisted the throttle and laid down some rubber. The truck turned out to be a triple rig. Kurt roared under the third section; it cut his head off. It happened right in front of the A & W, and Kurt's head rolled down the street in front of mom and pop and the kids, sitting there sipping away at root beer floats.

Just after this "accident" I left The Dalles for California, and for a ride of my own.

CHAPTER 3

I awoke in a long, dark, cool hallway where I lay for hours. At first I was only aware of voices and the chill in the air. Later I could make out, at the edge of my vision, a long line of patients on gurneys. Most seemed to be Mexicans or Negroes. I was flat on my back, I couldn't move a muscle, and I had no idea what was going on.

Finally a doctor loomed over me with an instrument that looked like a cross between a pizza cutter and a sharp, roweled spur. This he proceeded to run over various parts of my body. Could I feel that? No. Or anything over here? No. How about here? Nothing. So what was wrong with me?

"You're paralyzed."

"For how long?"

"Probably for life."

I did not feel the weight of those words at that time. I heard them, all right; but they held no more significance than *hello* or *good-bye*.

I was in the emergency unit at Long Beach Memorial Hospital, south of Los Angeles. When it was discovered that I had no insurance and would be a MediCal patient, I was put in an ambulance, braced with sandbags, and shipped north a dozen miles to Harbor General, a big public hospital in Torrance. I drifted in and out of consciousness. In the elevator to Harbor General's intensive care unit I told my parents, who had flown down from The Dalles, that I hoped my case would prove an example to other kids who would drink and drive. Fake bravado I would choke on for years afterward.

I couldn't figure out why I *felt* my legs to be flexed, as if I were sitting; when I looked at them, they were stretched out flat on the gurney in front of me.

Intensive care at Harbor General was on the twentieth floor. Five patients to a unit, with a panel of nurses monitoring telemetry from behind glass windows. Bright, bright lights. Surprisingly noisy, too. Very little peace and quiet for the dying or the nearly dying. The average survival time for my fellow inmates here was half a day.

They strapped me to a circle electric bed, in essence a chrome Ferris wheel bisected by a hard cot. For the prevention of bedsores, every two hours the bed would be rotated by a motor, leaving me facing either the floor or the ceiling. When I was facedown, my chin was supported by a canvas strap. A second stretcher would be strapped onto my back whenever it was time for the wheel to flip me belly-up. Every time my head passed the zenith, I experienced a tremendous anxiety attack. It was terrifying to feel myself blacking out as a result of all the blood draining out of my head. I'd scream, "Turn it faster! Speed it up!" They'd scream back, "We can't turn it faster!" The motor only ran at one speed.

In the facedown position it felt as if all my weight was supported on the chinstrap. I could do nothing about it, not even move so much as a fraction of an inch.

To hold my spine straight, I was fitted with Crutchfield tongs. Small holes were drilled in my skull, and the "tongs"—small screws with eyelets—were inserted. To these were fastened cables that ran over pulleys to attached weights. IVs were run into my arms, a nasogastric tube was shoved down my nose, and a catheter was rammed up my dick.

I would remain thus crucified for six weeks.

None of this apparatus worked perfectly. Quite often the needles pulled out of my arms during the rotation of the bed. One of the screws wrenched out of my skull in the dead of night, leaving all the weight supported by the other side, until the doctor in charge, furious with the incompetence of his interns, was summoned to replace it. The pain was extraordinary. As he twisted the screw back in, Dr. Malone could see my agony but could do nothing to relieve it. His anger and frustration were plain to see. The next night he came back to visit me. He put his hand on my shoulder. "Jesus Christ," he said, "my heart really goes out to you . . . twenty-one years old and probably paralyzed for life."

Tears ran down my face. I was touched that this fifty-five- or sixty-year-old doctor was letting the professional mask slip and being candid with me. Only later did his words sink in. I thought, Hey, wait a minute! The man clearly felt nothing could be done for me.

I ought to add that the screws were periodically removed so

that the holes could be sterilized. There was no way to anesthetize this. Fifteen years later I show my girlfriends the holes behind and above my temples, which still itch like crazy.

They kept me loaded to the gills with morphine or Demerol, and the days and nights ran together with none of the psychological relief that comes from a real sleeping-and-walking cycle. For me, I was unusually calm, or so I thought. The nurses remembered me, later on, as pretty feisty. "You're the type that survives, though."

The idea, implicit in Dr. Malone's pity, that I wouldn't get better, seemed incredible to me. I had always gotten out of jams. If nothing else worked, my father, always the Man in Charge, fixed things. If I was in really deep trouble, he put in a word here or a word there. But my parents, who had stayed for a week right after the accident, did not return during the rest of my six weeks in intensive care. Money was the reason given, but maybe this abandonment, which has haunted me ever since, had more to do with hopelessness: this was one situation that David Callahan couldn't fix.

Spiritual help was available in the person of a priest who made daily visits. By the time he got to me, I learned from the nurses, he had read the last rites and given extreme unction to about twenty people, which made him hollow-eyed and depressed-looking. He could have been something out of *The Exorcist*. Jesus, I thought, bring me a Hare Krishna priest instead.

Lying there, I remembered the priest who showed up at the deathbed of Foley's father. A cancer had spread from his mouth throughout his whole body, but Ed Foley never lost his Irish wit and ready sense of humor. I was there when The Dalles hospital chaplain came in, very solemn, and asked in a low, courteous tone, "Ed, would you like to speak with me at all?" Ed's mouth was too swollen for speech but he had a pencil and pad at his bedside. He scribbled a short note, tore the page off and gave it to the priest, who read it, nodded graciously, and walked gently out of the room.

Later, when Ed had drifted off into one of his little morphine naps, Foley and I were tidying up the room. I happened to pick up the note. It read, simply, "Hit the pike."

Even nailed to the wheel, wondering if I'd ever walk again, I tried to flirt with the nurses. There was a pair of cute little twins among the volunteers. But it wasn't enough that they were pretty and had big tits, they also had to turn out to be evangelical Christians! Once, one of them gently laid her hands on me "to release the demons from your spinal cord." I simultaneously prayed for the release of the demons in the buttons on her blouse.

In later years I came to understand that this was a fact of paralyzed life: I attract a lot of Christians. I look vulnerable, I'm in no position to refuse spiritual help, therefore I must be ready to accept Jesus. Recently a man approached me as I was taking the air in Pioneer Square, the center of downtown Portland. "Can I cure you?" he asked eagerly. "Jesus will help me cure you if you have enough faith."

I thought fast. "Gee," I said, "mind if I wait just a few months? I just got this wheelchair and it cost me five grand."

At Harbor General I was in the care of Dr. Wiles, an intern who resembled Columbo in a rumpled lab coat. Probably not yet out of his twenties, he was already slightly stooped over as if with the weight of his responsibilities. He was always hovering around me, checking the IVs, looking for bedsores, giving the nurses hell if they screwed up any of the apparatus. We became friendly, but he was determinedly professional and I couldn't get much out of him.

I couldn't get used to the lack of sensation. I felt nothing but my head and shoulderblades pressing on the hard slab beneath my back, or, on the other side, the top of my chest and my chin hitting the strap. I felt like a floating head.

The general din of the unit helped to distract me from the pain and panic that kept trying to surface. When not listening to the last screams of some person who had been crushed by a bus, or drifting in the haze of chemicals and spinal shock, my mind wandered in the past, seeking out childhood images.

The sunny summer sky outside the unit's lone window triggered memories of other Julys. It was customary in The Dalles for kids between the ages of eight and fourteen to get up before dawn in late summer and tramp the country lanes to pick fruit in the cherry orchards that covered the slopes of the Columbia Gorge just west of town. My brother Kit and I, along with several other boys, would already be hard at work when the eerie golden light of the summer dawn filtered through the trees.

The soft, powdery furrows of dirt underneath the trees went on forever. These orchards were truly vast—most of the cocktail cherries in the world came from them and the Bing cherry was named here, for a pioneer grower's Chinese foreman—but we boys, doing the first hard work of our lives, would have cared less about that, had we known. We felt very put upon to be out there slaving away.

The groves echoed with Spanish, shouted or sung. The colorfully dressed Mexican harvest workers seemed very exotic to me, singing their songs in the morning and stabbing each other in the sunset. I tended not to buy into the town's attitude toward them, which was one of extreme prejudice. Much as the townspeople hated and distrusted the Mexicans, though, their deepest loathing was reserved for the "white trash" transient pickers. Something must be horribly wrong with *Americans* who would work a job like that, went the logic. On another level, it was dispiriting to us kids to watch these experts outpick us at the rate of about four hundred buckets a minute.

I clearly remember my first bucket of cherries. It hadn't occurred to me that the fruit would rot if you didn't also pick the stem. So I just scooped the cherries off the tree, using my fingers like a rake, and had a bucketful in no time. I presented it to the orchardist, who made the rounds in an old army jeep. He took one look at the bucket, grabbed it away from me, dumped the cherries into the dirt and did a wild fandango on them, frothing with rage. I thought, Gee, that's a drag, if I have to pull the cherries by the stem it's going to take five times as long to fill the bucket.

Of course we ate about as many cherries as we picked, the inevitable result being massive cases of the trots. Our friend Ernest was tending to this problem when my brother Kip and I tipped the outhouse over with him inside. The contents of the tank spilled all over him, and he chased us down the hill, brown and angry.

Tricks like that were necessary to break up the monotony. By the time noon came and we could pull out our meager sandwiches, it felt like we'd been there for forty years. I would have taken a lot of those hours in trade for the ones I was passing now, after three weeks strapped to the wheel, with three more to go.

Every night on the intensive care ward, and for some reason always in the dead of night, I spiked a mysterious raging, potentially fatal fever. And every night Wiles, who seemed never to sleep, covered me with an electric "ice blanket." To the accompaniment of terrible spasms, my temperature was bludgeoned back down. They never diagnosed this fever.

Sometimes it seemed as if there was no color in the days and nights. Whites, grays, blacks. White coats, white sheets.

One night I woke up and, for a few seconds, didn't remember anything about the accident or where I was. I tried to move and when I found I couldn't, I felt an overwhelming panic, as would someone who had been buried alive or entombed in cement with barely enough room to flare his nostrils. And when I began to remember, the panic only got worse. Up to now, I had tried to be a tough guy, to hold in all the stress. But suddenly my inhibitions were broken down. I was finally shattered by all the strain, all the time I couldn't feel my goddamn legs, these tongs in my head, the lights of the ICU that never went off. It was more important that I move my legs than that the world survive.

I just told God, "I'm having a break, now. I'm going to stand up. I'm going to take five minutes. Just five minutes to run down and get some coffee, cross my legs, relax, take a deep breath. Somebody told me I had to stay here. That was last month! I can't even go out and have a cigarette. I'm not that stable to begin with! I want relief! I want a drink!"

But the only answer I got was silence. I began to scream my fucking lungs out: "GODDAMN IT HELP ME MOTHER-FUCK SOMEBODY HELP ME. . . ."

And there was somebody working that night, a big, black Aunt Jemima sort of woman. And she came over and she put her arms around me and rocked me like a baby. I screamed and screamed, and she just said, "Ah, there, honey, there, there." She just calmed me back down with her strength. It came through her skin. The strength of her skin. And I went back to sleep.

I always feared that this would happen again. I remembered Sister Joseph of Mary, back in The Dalles, who loved to talk about the martyrs. She loved to describe their torture in detail. An orgasmic look came over her face as she told how spears were shoved into their orfices, how hot stones were laid on them, how they were riddled with arrows or torn limb from limb, always turning to Christ *in extremis* so that their agony was, at the last, transformed into ecstasy. I couldn't imagine such certainty. I wasn't even sure who *I* was, let alone God. I often felt totally alone in the world, as if I were from a different planet. I didn't know then that this was a typical feeling of adoptees.

Often in intensive care I thought about my birth mother. I hated her for having given me up. You shit, you bitch, you were probably a thirteen-year-old who got knocked up in the back of a drive-in. But part of me felt worshipful toward this mysterious being, about whom I knew less than I did about the Mother of God.

A similar ambivalence governed my feelings about my family and tinged my already morbid thoughts of the future. The last thing I wanted was to be "a burden" to them. On the other hand, why weren't they here when I needed them?

I was usually kept naked. Too often, it seemed as if there were a couple of dozen Chinese medical students standing there, all shiny. Female medical students. "Uh, this is a twenty-one-year-old quadriplegic, with a complete cervical-six lesion, uh . . ." And they'd be looking with the sheets off, probing my genitals, shuffling my papers, tightening my screws, checking the wristband to make sure I was not an imposter trying to fake my way into quadriplegia.

People who acted like I was a human being were scarce. I made friends with Mrs. Leiberman, a middle-aged Jewish nurse's aide who brushed my teeth, gave me extra alcohol rubs, and became my champion against the nurses, with whom, as a person of inferior hospital status, she was at war anyway. We shared a loathing for the X-ray technicians, who always barged in and elbowed her aside without acknowledging her existence (or mine) to position their grotesque machine and ram their cold plates under my neck. Anybody who could walk got out when these demons appeared. The doctors were keeping close tabs on my vertebrae as they slowly aligned themselves under traction. Since my spinal cord had to be monitored daily, I got enough X radiation to grow a second head.

After four weeks an occupational therapist showed up, proudly displaying a device he had made for me. It was a mouth stick, with a kind of rubber fixture on one end. I was supposed to bite onto the rubber end and turn pages with it. This would make me an independent person all over again, back to normal, in control of my life. At the time I could do nothing for myself, and I was enthusiastic about the idea. My arms and hands were so swollen from hanging down that Dr. Wiles was afraid my rings—I had been wearing three of the silly things at the time of the accident—would cut off circulation and I'd lose three of my fingers. He put wristbands on so that my arms could be hoisted up into the sleepwalking position and so that the fingers might deflate; due to spinal shock the fingers stayed as fat as a pack of bad franks, however. Finally Wiles got a jeweler's saw and cut the rings off.

At the beginning of the swing shift, in late afternoon, I was given a high-calorie drink, something like a malted, to gain weight. I could drink this myself, through a straw, but dinner had to be spoon-fed. The aide would tilt the circle bed up a little for a better angle, and then she'd sit there chatting with her buddy across the desk in some unknown language while absently shoveling peas into my mouth. To get the boring job over with, she'd go faster and faster until, chew as fast as I might, I could no longer keep up. I'd start to spray the food back out: "Good God, you stupid cunt, you want me to fuckin' choke to death? Slow down!"

The big event of my day came in the evening, when the circle electric bed would be wheeled over to the window so that I could watch the sunset. As night fell, thoughts of hopelessness began to well up. I prayed. I made my promises. I remembered all the promises to God and the pacts with the Devil made by characters in literature to escape horrible fates. And here I was. I said, "God, I just can't be paralyzed. Things always work out for John Callahan. Ed Foley comes to bail me out when I'm caught driving drunk. My dad gets things 'squared away.' There's got to be some way out of this. John Callahan is *not* one of the ones who ends up paralyzed."

I nerved myself up to ask Wiles. "Do you think I'm making any progress? What kind of progress can I expect?"

"It's really hard to say for certain at this time."

I sensed through Wiles's carefully even, flat tone that the curtain had already fallen for me.

At night I distracted myself with erotic thoughts about Marisa, the night-duty nurse whom I occasionally talked into giving me extra pain shots. At night she and her colleagues turned some of the lights out, a bit of relief from the bright white walls, white ceiling, white uniforms, and white lab coats. White became the very color of pain itself for me and turned me into a night-dweller forever afterward. Down the dark corridor a desk lamp at the nurses' station highlighted the curve of Marisa's cheek and suggested her voluptuous body. Often in intensive care the ghosts of old girlfriends visited my drifting mind to point accusing fingers at old wrongs. I had been a failure in all my relationships, I knew. Perhaps what I longed for was contained in this fleeting night image of Marisa: an unattainable woman, wrapped in shadows.

One night, unable to sleep, I convinced her to wheel me out into the corridor for a smoke. Marisa lit the cigarette for me in her own mouth and held it to my lips. I took a long, luxurious draw and waited for the relief. But something went wrong. The cigarette reacted with my central nervous system, and the sentient part of my body—from the nipples up—was consumed in fiery pain. It was perfect aversion therapy. If I ever find out what really happened, I'll sell the information to the Schick Centers for the Control of Smoking. At the time, I felt overwhelming panic, as I had when I just *had* to move, but, of course, couldn't. Angel Marisa calmed me, eventually.

Was this the way things were going to be? Better ignorance than that kind of knowledge, better hope than truth. After five weeks in intensive care I still hadn't asked anybody how I was pissing or shitting.

All this time I existed in a social milieu of people so badly mangled they were playing "musical respirators." I especially remember one woman who had been run over by a truck and who had a brain injury. They were just waiting for her to die. She managed to pull her catheter out and whip it around in a circle, spraying us all with pee before giving up the ghost. Terminal stabbing cases, gunshot wounds. . . . I used to wake up and look out the window at the dawn and think, "Gee, what a *glorious* day to be hovering between life and death."

One afternoon in my third week of intensive care a woman had come into the room, crossed to the corner by the window where I was strapped to the circle bed, said "Hi, I am Annu," and sat down. A lovely blonde Swedish or Norwegian woman in her early thirties who resembled (in retrospect) Daryl Hannah, Annu wore a pretty blue summer dress. She had deep blue pools for eyes, and spoke with a strong accent when she spoke at all. I liked her immediately and found myself pouring my heart out to her. Often her side of our conversations was limited to, "So what else?"

Annu came every day, including weekends and days off. She would sit on the floor if I was facedown, so that we were always face to face.

"Hi, John. How are you?"

"Ah, fucked. I'm doing badly today. One of the goddamn nurses spilled peas all down my neck. I had a fight with the head nurse when I tried to get an alcohol rub. I'm uncomfortable. I don't even know how I piss. It's driving me crazy! I want out of this place!"

"Yah, yah, it doesn't sound like it's going too well."

"It's awful. I don't know how I can go on. I just don't know how I'm going to have a future at all. The doctors don't tell me but it looks like I'm going to be like this for life."

"John, you're a special person. I know you can make it. I feel it."

"I just don't know. I just don't know. I'm going crazy."

We would both cry. And how I loathed having all the goddamn slimeball nurses in this tiny little ICU all able to see this tender soap-opera thing between us. I couldn't even have a moment alone to go crazy with my new friend.

"I got you some flowers. I hope you like them."

"Yes. Just put them on the windowsill there."

"Would you like me to rub your back?"

"Yes."

"It's a lovely day out. It's very hot. I drove here in my convertible."

I could just imagine this beautiful blonde with the sexy smile driving her convertible in the sun down the Hollywood Freeway from Santa Monica to visit me, to talk to me in her soft voice about nonsensical things I can barely remember.

"Do you think I'm still good-looking?"

"You are a very good-looking young man. That hasn't changed. You have tremendous strength. I know it. You will go on."

I was comforted. From anybody else I would have thought this was total bullshit. I believed Annu. I knew that I was becoming dependent on her, that I was putting all my emotional eggs into her basket. It was that or go nuts.

Tactfully, Annu never said much about herself. I gathered that her husband worked on an offshore oil rig and that they had no kids. When, after six weeks in the ICU, it was decided that I was stable enough to leave intensive care and move on to a rehabilitation center, she came to say good-bye. And that was that. I never saw her again and I wonder sometimes if she really wasn't just a dream. She was an angel, anyway.

RANCHO LOS AMIGOS Hospital, fifteen miles away in Downey, California, was one of the largest and most advanced rehabilitation centers in the world. Almost from the moment I regained consciousness after the accident, the aides, and especially Mrs. Hasson, were coaching me to "try for Rancho" in preference to Encino, where there was another, lesser facility. They made it sound like getting into Harvard. So I never failed to mention Rancho when talking to doctors or senior staff. After a while everyone simply assumed I was going to Rancho, and that's the way it went down on my chart.

By the end of my stay in intensive care I had become exceedingly restless. I knew by then that I was going to have to live in a wheelchair. I remembered movies I'd seen: it was perhaps cool to be in a wheelchair, had a certain dashing style. But, I saw no future as a ceiling tile expert. It would be a definite improvement to see the world in the vertical once more, to trade my belly-button perspective for life at areola level. So I was excited when they put on a gurney, strapped and braced into position, and loaded into an ambulance. But I wasn't exactly headed toward a wheelchair—at least not yet.

A week before I left, Wiles explained to me that I would have to have an operation to strengthen and stabilize my spine; there was no hope of improvement, but the operation would prevent further damage. One of the benefits of going to Rancho was that this procedure would be done by a world-famous expert, the hospital's director, Dr. Emile Stahlmaster. Performed shortly after my arrival at Rancho Los Amigos, it was called a cervical anterior fusion. The smashed vertebrae were reinforced with bone taken from my hip. To bear the weight of my head, the transplanted bone had to be installed on the front side of the spine. Dr. Stahlmaster had to more or less disassemble my neck to get there. He had done the same thing, I was told, for George Wallace.

On my third morning at Rancho they gave me a shot and I began to fade away. I remember feeling very cold. I fought the anesthesia, fought the feeling of control slipping away from me, screaming and floundering around. Finally I passed out.

I woke up in stages, as if I were a swimmer rising from a deep dive into a deep lake. First was darkness. Then, ever so slowly, light above. Then shapes, perhaps the roots of trees at the water's edge. And then breaking the thin membrane of the surface into a blind, bright world that was mostly made up of pain. I felt tremendous pain and thirst. I saw what looked like waves, waves of white linen passing across my vision. White curtains being drawn around me, white doctors.

I couldn't speak to tell anybody of the horrible thirst. A thick plastic tube—an airway—had been rammed down my throat to keep me from choking to death during the operation and I couldn't communicate anything. That frightened me badly.

I slept and woke and slept and woke. When I woke for good, I realized that I had been better off asleep. A nurse finally came by and pulled the airway out of my throat. Every couple of hours she explained that I was being turned on a turning sheet— "logrolled," in hospital jargon—so that my neck, now caught in a stiff brace, would not move in relation to any part of my body. I yearned to kick my feet, to move any limb at all to distract myself from this torture in my neck. I couldn't. I asked for water and was given nothing. I was getting water in an IV, they told me. I might choke. It was three days before I was allowed some ice chips.

The pain reduced my sleep periods to short, nightmare-filled dozes. I dreamed about my friend Tad Jamison, a baseball prodigy on a Little League team, six feet four inches tall even at age twelve. He was a pitcher *and* he always hit a home run. At age thirteen he had hung himself from a water pipe in his father's basement workshop, using a dog leash. In my dream I saw Tad's swollen face, heard him scream, saw him kick. Every time I got another pain shot, and passed out again, I'd have this dream.

I experienced the stretching of time all sufferers of truly intolerable pain report. During the worst of my six weeks in Harbor General I had never once contemplated suicide. Now I sincerely wanted to die.

Even that passed.

When, after several days, I managed to half emerge from my

drugged state, a guy carrying a clipboard wearing a tweed jacket, a knit tie, and a goofy grin came by.

"Hi, I'm Wally Green from Public Relations! As it happens, I actually witnessed your entire neck surgery. Yep, I actually saw your neck wide open. The whole damn thing! It was really interesting. Boy, I'll tell you, what they can do nowadays. . . ."

CHAPTER 4

"The latest in adaptive equipment."

After a week they transferred me from bed to yet another gurney and wheeled me across the Rancho parking lot to Ward 6, Cervical Injuries.

Rancho Los Amigos occupies a campus bigger than my hometown, huge building after huge building joined by palm-lined walks and formal gardens. Enormous wards catered to each category of maim: spinals, head injuries, amputees, deformed children, werewolf-bite victims. In my day, there was even an airplane hangar's worth of iron-lungers, people too smashed up to do their own breathing.

My room on Ward 6 looked like the set of *The Men*, except that Marlon Brando was nowhere in sight. The rest of the cast was perfect, though: two whites, two Hispanics, one black, one Japanese, and one American Indian. It was an ACLU attorney's dream.

For the first time, after eight weeks laid out alone on a marble slab, I witnessed animation again. People were vibrant, as quads and paraplegics often are on these wards. People with real wills rolled in and out at tremendous speeds. Running around with the sidebars of their chair seats casually left off. Slapping palms against the doorjamb to make the chairs cut sharp turns. Flying into the rooms on two wheels, grabbing stuff out of lockers and roaring back to wherever they were headed, laughing, swearing, and kidding one another. Even one guy driving an electric wheelchair with his mouth!

The patients were buzzing the nurses, who were dressed in bright lime-green or champagne-pink blouses over their white slacks. The nurses were barking at the guys in ward vernacular. "Get the fuck down here, Willy. You know you got O.T. Hey, get back and clean this mess up. Get out of here and grab some P.T.— lookit, it's sunny out there!"

Holy shit, maybe I'll be active like this, I thought.

A dark-haired girl rolled up with an aggressively cheerful, "Hi! I'm Debbie!" She was dressed for success in a sharp navy outfit with tie, and was from the front office. In spite of the wheelchair, she looked plenty able. Maybe there *was* life after a broken back.

If so, it was a ways off. In addition to my neck brace I had to wear a diaphragm across my stomach, support hose, and splints to stiffen my wrists. Once this exoskeleton was on, I could be attached to a Hoyer lift and hoisted into a chair for the first time. I think I lasted five or six minutes before passing out. It took two weeks to build up enough sitting tolerance to last the four to six hours necessary for the therapy program to begin. In that time my body literally relearned the habit of supplying my brain with blood.

It was amazing to see the world from an upright position, to regain normal lateral vision after two months without so much as a pillow. I felt like a kid on the first day of high school, a total outsider. I had to make it into this clique.

I am a C5-6 quadriplegic, which means that my spinal cord is severed between the fifth and sixth vertebrae counting down from the top. That's about halfway between decathalon champion and rigor mortis. I can work my triceps, half of my deltoids, half of my diaphragm. If I don't watch it, I can choke to death. I can extend my fingers, but not close them around a fork or a pen. Everything from my diaphragm down is without sensation and, naturally, beyond voluntary control.

Paraplegics, by contrast, are people injured lower on the spine. They have the use of all or most of their upper bodies and can play, for example, wheelchair basketball. Any C5-6 would love to be a paraplegic and, at the same time, is grateful not to have been injured high enough to rate an iron lung. Yes, quads wish they were paras, paras wish they were able-bodied, and the able-bodied wish they were Jane Fonda.

Quite a bit of the curriculum at Rancho involves getting the autonomic nervous system to take over bodily functions that were formerly controlled by the brain. Say, for example, you want to take a pee. If you are able-bodied, your bladder signals that it is full. Excusing yourself from your board meeting, you head for the toilet. Only when safely astride the porcelain throne, or before the marble magnificence of the urinal, does your brain permit the appropriate muscle to relax and the stream to issue forth.

But the para or quadriplegic does not sense when his or her bladder is full. There is no mental command to loose or to bind, as convenience dictates. Each quad or paraplegic is at first fitted with an "indwelling" catheter to route urine that is being passed at random intervals. This device must be installed and removed by a trained person, so it is desirable to replace it with a Texas catheter: a condom with a tube attached. But that can't happen until the bladder itself is trained to empty itself at predictable intervals. At Rancho that was the job of the Dick Police.

I don't know what the women with spinal injuries called them, but for me the urology technicians, mounted on speedy golf carts equipped with racks of pee bags and catheters, remained the Dick Police. Their mission: to seek out every quad and para according to his or her schedule, catheterize, unclamp, empty and reclamp each and every bladder until such time as it autonomously stayed shut until called upon to open.

Naturally we tried to outwit the Police, but they were an elite corps, astoundingly efficient. Once, I parked my chair in a remote supply closet behind seven gurneys piled high with blankets. Hell, I thought, they'll never get me. However, minutes later, they hit. The door flew open, the light snapped on. Zip, the dick came out. Zip, in went the catheter. And zip, they were gone. Cutting the tape, Nurse Robbie clicked his scissors at me mockingly. "It won't be long now, Callahan!"

Other simple human functions required special attention as well: at age twenty-one, I taught myself to eat.

I was left alone in a wheelchair in the lunchroom one morning with a bowl of cereal on my lap. Maybe I was late, or maybe the therapists simply didn't want to watch. My neck was rigidly braced, so I could see the bowl only as a blur on the edge of my peripheral vision. My wrists were in heavy plaster casts to stabilize the tendons until I regained some muscular strength. A spoon was stuck through a spring fastener on the right cast.

When I thought I had some cereal in the spoon, I started to bring it up. But my arm was trembling so much as I tried to coordinate my muscles to bring it to my mouth that the cereal shook off the spoon.

After several more attempts, I dropped the spoon into the cereal and a geyser of milk splattered up into my face. And as I let my arms fall, I could not feel them contact the armrests of the chair.

I thought, This is the way it's going to be for the rest of my life. I can't even feed myself. I can't shit or piss for myself. I can't have a woman. I can't get in or out of my wheelchair and I can't even push it effectively.

The wheelchair was, so far, a big disappointment. I thought I would be able to zip around and have some freedom. But I was so weak that it took me an exhausting half hour just to get down the hall, a distance of fifty yards. Much less negotiate the miles and miles of similar halls, each half a football field long that ran throughout the huge complex.

There in the lunchroom, dripping with sticky milk, the utter strangeness of it swept over me as if it had all started five minutes before. I was a head stitched to a dead body. I was living my life in a hopeless situation, in a doorless six-bed room with a bunch of goons and nurses sweeping in and out as they pleased. I couldn't go out and see my friends. I missed my friends. I missed my family.

I felt the tears begin to run down my face. I thought, Jesus Christ in heaven, let a lightning bolt strike me fucking down.

Julio Gomez, a ward mate who was a heroin addict and had been shot in the neck during an L.A. gang war, didn't want to learn to feed himself. Julio put his face down in the bowl. "I'll eat like a fucking dog, man."

When I was able to sit up in the chair long enough, I began two hours of physical therapy and two of occupational therapy daily. The latter included feeding, grooming, and dressing. I remember having my hands harnessed for long periods of time to a rolling-pin-like apparatus that sanded a piece of wood. A bright future as a finish sander stretched before me if I played my cards right.

Physical therapy was more inspiring. Since my body would now have to be hauled around, dressed, maneuvered in and out of bed, made love to and so forth without voluntary control, it would need to be capable of extraordinary flexibility. I was strapped to a tilt table, a padded board about four feet off the ground, fitted with a footrest to keep me from sliding off. A leg would be splinted and attached to a rope coming down from a pulley on the ceiling. Then the rope would be tightened and the leg pulled up as, simultaneously, the table was tilted down. A few more inches every day. If I'd been able to feel it, I would have confessed to heresy or anything else after a few seconds; instead, after an hour of this daily for six months, my hamstrings were so abnormally stretched that I could have stuffed my toes in my ears. If I could have moved them.

I couldn't feel the pain of the actual stretching; but I *could* feel "dysreflexia," a response that included sweating, chills, headaches and spasms in my back muscles.

When not wondering when the therapist would actually succeed in pulling off my leg, I watched the scene in the huge gym, where paraplegics learned to transfer in and out of their chairs, quads practiced rolling on the forty-by-fifty-foot elevated mat, people in leg braces learned to walk, all under the supervision of a perfectly conditioned staff.

My therapist, Chuck Wilson, commuted to Alabama, where he put Governor Wallace to similar torture. "Come on, tell me about Wallace," I kept asking. No matter how I pleaded, though, he never let fall a single word on the subject. Either he was professionally discreet or he was afraid some of the governor's supporters might burn a cross on his front lawn.

My second therapist was an attractive woman named Mary Mills. I really looked forward to rolling around on the mat with Mary, whose years in the gym had given her the ideal California hardbody.

Among many other things she taught me transfers, the art of getting from chair to bed, couch, car seat, and so on, unassisted. For this the quadriplegic uses a "transfer" board, not unlike a skateboard without the wheels and about the same size. I learned to shove one end under my ass and place the other on the destination surface, in this case the elevated wrestling mat. Then I would stiffen my elbows and use the heels of my hands to scoot myself across the board. Since this involved balance it was especially hard to do with my rigid neck brace, still on a month after my operation, which prevented me from shifting most of the weight that was still available to shift—my head.

The final P.T. element was weight training, and, in keeping with the general theme of bondage, I pumped my iron via ropes, pulleys and a set of Velcroed handcuffs.

A couple of times a week I wheeled down to the orthotics department where, at great expense, a set of custom-fitted wrist splints was being developed for me. These were spring-loaded to increase the force of my grip. I would have great silver claws! I wanted to take them out to the Mojave and try them out on a dead jackal. Later on, living in the real world, I would find these Bionic Man gadgets embarrassing; eventually I threw them away.

Too bad most quads are broke. What a market for souped-up wheelchairs, electric beds, sixty-thousand-dollar adapted vans, remote-controlled lifts. . . . The very cushion my sensationless behind sits on is a three-hundred-dollar item. Bedsores can liter-

ally kill you. If unchecked, changes in the cells occur that lead to osteomyelitis, degenerative bone disease. The sores are a constant threat when the body can't feel itself being abraded, can't shift its position to get relief it can't even appreciate anyway. "Death Row" at Rancho was a ward devoted to people with hopeless bedsores. Sometimes I went down to look at it when I had nothing better to do. It seemed aptly named.

An hour every other day was spent in sex therapy. I didn't want to go until I saw the counselor, Margie Bighew, Ph.D., a plump but sensuous Germanic-looking woman who operated out of a tiny windowless cubicle. The place was so small that it seemed as if my nose was between her sizable breasts as she interrogated me with such lines as, "Have you thought about asking that little nurse of yours to sit on your face some night, John?"

A shocking yet wildly exciting thought! The idea of sex was frightening. What was I capable of? Besides, I was still medicated: 10 milligrams of Valium every four hours between me and a mass of fears and insecurities. Still . . .

Dr. Bighew was a great believer in spontaneous behavior. This was, after all, southern California, where either you were sexy or you were asked to leave the state. Still, I sometimes wondered if the doctors and other staff were aware of the exact nature of her advice.

"Why not play a little grab-ass with the nurses? You could always say, 'It was a wild spasm—sorry!'"

Maybe I *should* try to make a move. Nah, I was too embarrassed. At the same time I had fantasies of ripping off Margie's blouse, shoving my face between her tits, and making motorboat noises.

One-on-one in her office, she explained the mechanics of quad sex.

"You don't have ordinary, psychogenic erections anymore so you have to use reflexogenic erections. You've got to put your hands on your stomach just above your pubic area. You massage there and also the inner part of your thigh until you find the correct spot for that day." I was hoping she'd demonstrate. Instead, she used charts.

"You've got to think of sex differently. Maybe you're not the passive type, but you'll probably have to have intercourse from the bottom. But the girl will like it anyway because that provides better penetration."

Of course you can't talk to a twenty-one-year-old like that and not have the hormones pounding away in his ears. Once she did touch my neck to indicate new erogenous zones. Boy, its a good thing I'm paralyzed or I'd jump right out of this chair and pull her down, I thought. She'd probably touched hundreds if not thousands of other quads and paras the same way, but she certainly did revive my interest in the topic.

In spite of Margie Bighew I was convinced I was out to pasture as far as sex was concerned. I remember reading an article by Larry Flynt, the publisher of *Hustler*, who was paralyzed by a bullet. He had gone on at some length about how anyone with a spinal injury who said he had a decent sex life was a liar.

My occupational therapist was dismayed one day when she found me scrawling a doggerel poem in writing class:

All the same, I was twenty-one and I had got to be good friends with a girl who worked the graveyard shift. We made a lunch date. We explored the grounds, went by the fountain and behind the bushes a little bit. She was very sweet. Scared as I was, I invited her to sit in my lap; I had no idea that this was going to be my M.O. for the rest of my life. She was eager.

Two seconds into the first kiss my foot pedal broke under our combined weight. She fell flat on her ass on the ground and I followed. I cracked my head sharply against the chair, looked up at her, and said, "Now I know that God doesn't mean for me to have sex ever again."

Another part of sex therapy consisted of porn flicks showing quads and paras making it with normal girls (there were no comparable films for women in those days). These were the brainchildren of Dr. Sidney Shimkin, urologist. Perhaps Dr. Shimkin had enlisted the support of hard-core movie moguls, or maybe he was just an advanced student of the genre. The films, at least the ones I saw, were grainy, underlit, and complete with rinky-dink canned organ music on the sound tracks, just as boring and depressing as the real thing. One of them showed a quad turning a neat somersault to transfer himself from wheelchair to bed (applause) but in general they were gritty and humorless enough to put anybody off sex for years.

The final item on Rancho's basic curriculum was driver education—this was L.A. after all. Every other Friday I practiced in a 1966 pink Caddy equipped with a hand throttle and a knob on the power steering wheel. I had no idea at all how to keep my balance in this pimpmobile. Once, while out for a practice spin, I signaled a left turn, cranked the wheel over and fell directly into my instructor's lap. The Caddy lurched slowly up onto the sidewalk and into a bunch of kids on tricycles. They were too young to read the huge "Caution—Maimed Student Driver" signs on the roof. Luckily nobody was hurt.

The real education occurred between classes, however, as always. We hung on every word of the veterans who visited us, like Larry, a tough para, with a hugely muscled torso above his shrunken child legs, and with racing stripes on his wheelchair. Larry would whip into the ward with his perky, fully-abled wife on his lap. They took me to dinner. "I do anything anybody else does," he told me. "I go up escalators."

He did, too. He would drive on, lock his back wheels quickly, and lean forward to keep his chair from falling over backward.

Sometimes when he talked to me, he would thrust his chair backward toward the wall, lock his wheels at just the right moment and end up in a comfortable reclining position with his head against the wall. Fascinating.

"Don't limit yourself by what these therapists tell you—you can't do this, can't do that. Take what they have to offer but realize you can learn a lot more on your own."

Larry demonstrated self-defense, spinning his chair so that a burly attendant, dancing and faking and weaving, couldn't get in a punch. For tougher situations he owned a gun and knew how to use it. He drove a car, held a full-time job as an accountant, went to nude beaches, you name it.

What about sex? "Every night. I've even learned how to ejaculate."

He and his wife had been married, happily, for five years. She was motherly toward me, took me shopping. Once I saw them leaving the hospital together holding hands. Larry could push his chair and still manage to hold hands. I was very moved by this sight.

"But," I protested to him once, "you're a *para*plegic."

"Look," was all he said. Across the hall was a guy in an iron lung. Other people would feed him for the rest of his life. I became a fighter early on.

At the opposite extreme was Sonny, a guy on my ward who decided to opt out. He spent every free moment with one ear against the pillow and the other shielded from reality by a transistor-radio earplug. His aunt and uncle visited every weekend, but since Sonny was a case of abject despondency, they adopted me instead. I had few visits from relatives, and Sonny's came in handy. They brought me presents and much encouragement.

Somewhere in the middle was Elwood "You-wanna-buy-some-red-debbles?" Green, whose 13-year-old current wife showed up every weekend with an entourage of two dozen or so brats from Elwood's several previous marriages and a care package with Elwood's weekend supply of Mad Dog wine and mixed narcotics. "Git that one off da bed!" he would snap, between chugs. Elwood spent all his time on his stomach poling a gurney along the corridors with a crutch, as if it were a canoe, buying and selling whatever he could get his hands on. He had to use the gurney because, still in rehab, he had already developed chronic bedsores on his ass.

Of all the guys on the ward, I was most fond of Julio Gomez. After eight or ten weeks on the ward, I felt like a big brother to him. Only eighteen, he was very brave. His gunshot injury had paralyzed him on one side only, but had also left him with tremendous neural pain, which he hid during the day behind a big stoned grin. They medicated him heavily at night to stop him from screaming in his sleep.

Julio was born in the Philippines, but had grown up on the streets of East L.A. His mother, who he said was an alcoholic, visited him only once. Julio had never been taught a life of the mind: the gang scene depended on animal macho. "How you gonna load a gun with one arm?" he asked me once. He had lost everything that counted in his world.

When Julio's friends took him out, he would return with Xs in his eyes, zonked on heroin and booze. At other times he got his stuff from Elwood. We were all rough on women but Julio was rougher. Some young nurse would say, "Time to get up, Julio." And he'd say, "Fuck you, I ain't gettin' up. Get out of here, bitch."

The young nurse would go off in tears to Cathy Ball, the head nurse. Cathy would give Julio a lecture. "Julio, you're in here on welfare. We could easily throw you out." So Julio would get up and go down to therapy and, half an hour later, throw his hand splint across the room.

Julio never gave an inch. One day he went down to the cafeteria, which was staffed by the mentally retarded, and ordered seventeen cups of coffee. Julio grinned at me as the guy filled up his tray. Mean, but hilarious.

Sometimes I'd see him sitting out on the grass with the light gone out of his eyes and think, He's not gonna make it. Julio finally O.D.d. His friends on the outside shot him up. Maybe they thought he'd be better off that way.

My own role model was Will, in his late twenties, a good-looking, cynical para who kept a bottle in his locker, chain-smoked, and told no lies to himself or others. He was blatantly angry about his injury and had absolutely no illusions about what it meant for the future. He hated rehab. "These fucking doctors and nurses don't know what the fuck they're doin'," he'd growl, pouring me a shot of Scotch on his bedside table.

Cathy Ball would turn up in the doorway, tactfully ignoring the illegal booze. "Now, Will, you know you're in the most modern rehab center in the entire world. And you want to leave it?"

"Fuckin-A right!"

"You'll be sorry. You'll get bedsores, you won't learn to drive or do transfers, you won't have the skills to live on your own."

"Hell, I can learn all that stuff by myself. Get me the hell out of here. I'll get my damn lawyer in if you want me to."

Anger was the cork in the bottle of our repressed emotions. Any woman got a hard time; none more so than the nurse we called Tiny T, because she was a three-hundred-pounder who limped like a gunshot elephant. Hiroki was an athletic, independent para who'd go up and down the halls cutting wheelies in his chair. He hated confinement, so he'd keep the chair by his bed at night, which was strictly forbidden. When Tiny T tried to get it away from him, he wouldn't let go, and the whale-like nurse just about dragged him off the bed to a chorus of "Ah, fuck you, Tiny T!" One day Elwood Green asked, "You hate me, don't you, Tiny T?" and she answered, "I don't hate you. I just dislike you intensely."

Julio Gomez liked to fuck with Tiny T. "Yeah, Tiny T," he told her one night, "I'm loaded on reds. What the fuck you gonna do about it? I feel like I'm on the ceiling looking right down on you, you wrinkled old sow."

But Tiny T was no fool. She knew where Julio got the reds. She strode across the room and ripped open Elwood Green's locker. A pharmacy full of pills fell out. Elwood sat up on his bedsore-covered ass and tried to clobber Tiny T with his crutch, while the rest of the guys yelled, "You bitch, get the fuck out of here, we *all* got pills in our lockers!" So Tiny T ran around as fast as a seventy-five-year-old with elephantiasis could and busted everybody's stash—pot, downers, speed—none of which she had trouble locating. All I lost were some hoarded sleeping pills, chloral hydrate; but Elwood lost about five thousand dollars' worth of drugs. Even his shoes were full of them.

Any new staff got tested by the guys on the ward, and the acid test was bowel program. Six men in bed are turned on their sides, given laxative suppositories and supplied with diapers. I remember Martha, one young beginner who flunked. After a couple of hours the room smelled like a hog pen. Martha returned from an impromtu sprint to the can to face a double barrage of hooting sarcasm and unbearable stench. She turned on her heel, marched straight to the front desk, and resigned.

Not long after this incident, *Love Story* was featured as the weekly movie. From all sides came the sound of sobs and sniffles.

There in the dark these tough customers were crying. I found myself subject to frequent weeping triggered by the most trivial things.

At Christmas the kids from the children's ward, in their tiny wheelchairs and dressed in Santa costumes, came by at bedtime to carol us. Their little legs were like commas suspended beneath their twisted bodies. Whatever self-pity we were wallowing in was, for a moment anyway, erased.

Maybe because I was a compulsive extrovert, I was chosen by the hospital P.R. as a model quad, the guy to have on stage at fundraisers or to introduce to visiting bigwigs. I was not averse to putting on a suit and getting the extra attention. A P.R. guy and I would share the microphone and he'd say, "This is John Callahan, a C five-six quadriplegic. This is the kind of wheelchair he needs. He has this mobility . . ." And I would show the kind of strength I had in my hands and arms, do a transfer onto a sofa, and then answer questions.

I never really knew what they were pitching for, but I can guess that on at least one occasion they struck out. Ronald Reagan was the guest of honor. He was then engaged, as governor, in shrinking California's welfare rolls. Later he returned to haunt me, indirectly, as the inspirer of catch-22 welfare regulations that made it nearly impossible for people like me to earn our own living. At the time, though, I barely knew who the guy was.

Usually I would answer questions, sounding upbeat about Rancho. At one performance I showed a cartoon I'd scratched in occupational therapy. It showed two heads mounted on skid carts at the street corner. In front of each head was cup with pencils for sale. One of the heads was blind. The other head said, "People like you are a real inspiration to me."

"Kind of gloomy, don't you think?" asked one visiting M.D.

My real attitude toward Rancho was that I didn't want to get kicked out early, the way addicts were when they were caught; but at the same time I didn't accept the prescribed life-style. I spent the occupational therapy sessions writing poetry and drawing cartoons. And I was learning how to drink again, beginning with Will's Scotch, Elwood's Mad Dog, a couple of six-packs on the weekend. It wasn't much at first, but combined with the Valium it began to reintroduce me to the wonderful, isolated world of feeling no pain. Oddly enough, though, I hadn't consciously missed the stuff.

I was now allowed out of hospital during my free time. When my brothers came down to visit me at Christmas, we went out to a bar and I got blasted and maudlin. I told combat gags that I had written in occupational therapy:

Hey, I haven't had a chance to stand up all day.
I'm hoping to catch walking pneumonia.
These car accidents aren't all they're cracked up to be.
I suffer from motion sickness: it makes me sick that I can't move.

In my fourth month at Rancho my attorneys won a settlement in connection with the accident. I could go out to the 7-Eleven now for a six-pack whenever I felt like it.

One day the urge struck me as I was sunning myself in the courtyard, dressed only in a towel. So I wheeled across the lawn and across the two-lane road toward the 7-Eleven, a half-hour trip each way. I had just gotten up onto the grass lane divider when the towel caught in my spokes and whipped off my lap, jamming the chair's wheel. I waited for ages, stark naked in the middle of the road at eleven o'clock in the morning, before some passerby took pity on me and pulled out the towel. Thank God this was *southern* California.

At the end of six months it was time to graduate to life in the big world with an attendant, something I had been dreading for weeks. A social worker named Fanny Gridley was in charge of this step. She was a genuinely tough customer, with a massive jaw and a peg leg that looked like it might be useful for churning butter. She would have looked about right lashed to Moby Dick, giving him the spear as they went down for the last time.

Fanny had the mountainous job of lining up the social-support services for all of us. No one gave her even a hint of the shit we handed out to everybody else. When I would piss and moan about having to leave and how scared I was, she'd say, "Life is Major League, my friend."

Fanny didn't approve of Elwood Green, but she was far too professional to show it. She would just look at Elwood as he poled his way up the hall with his mouth sagged open and his eyes blank, goofing on God knows what chemical. Once I heard her mutter, "Elwood Green. What are we gonna do with you?"

She never really lightened up around anybody, but she certainly understood quads and paras. One morning all six of us decided not to get up. We were going on permanent strike because the staff would only give us one "green tub" bath a month. This involved lifting the bather with a crane into a real tub instead of the usual bed bath. We felt that Rancho could do better.

When Fanny heard about us, she walked across the hall from her little bare office and said, "You bunch of big babies! Get on your asses and get going!" We did. She worked hundreds of extra hours for us, and more for the impossible cases like Julio Gomez, and we knew it.

One other noteworthy thing happened before I left Rancho.

It was a weekend, my next-to-last in the rehab center, and I was alone in the room. My five roommates had gone on pass. It was near midnight, I was sitting up in bed watching TV with my curtain drawn around me. A nurse I had never seen before came in. She was what was called a floater; she replaced whatever nurse had to miss a shift.

When she came in, I happened to be playing with myself. I had a reflexogenic erection. I was caught without anything on and, needless to say, I was not able to quickly reach for a sheet to cover myself up.

"Would you like some help with that?" she asked.

As I remember, she had dark hair, was kind of Italian-looking, sexy, probably a decade or so older than me. She leaned over the side of the bed and began to give me a blow job. Perhaps the rest of the nurses were gone from the ward on a break so that she felt safe; maybe she was just crazy. I was happy about it either way.

Then she opened her dress, pulled down her panties, climbed up on the bed, and mounted me, pouring out her beautiful breasts into my face as she did so. After about fifteen minutes she just pulled away, asking me if I needed more water or perhaps a sleeping pill. Then she was gone. I never saw her again. At the time, I couldn't believe this had happened. Later, I would find out it was commonplace.

In Fanny Gridley's office soon thereafter I finally had to face an introduction to Al Muller, my first live-in attendant. He was a tall, overweight man with dyed black hair, a goatee, and a sour, tight-assed smirk. I noticed he had an uneven gait as he walked down the hall with Fanny; I felt like asking him if he wanted to steady himself on my wheelchair.

However, I was determined not to be a burden to my family. Here was the person I'd be living with for the foreseeable future.

I had an awful sense of fear and apprehension. I'd actually been trying to delay my release from Rancho, because I knew the party would really be over once I was away from the support system of the ward. Now I was sure it would.

Al got a week of training at Rancho before the inevitable morning when he pushed me, suitcase on my lap, across the parking lot to his old Dodge. As we set out on the four-mile drive to his apartment in an industrial slum in Santa Ana, he turned his vodka breath on me and asked, "You like auto racing?"

CHAPTER 5

Al's apartment in Santa Ana resembled the honeymoon suite in a cheap motel. I was the unwilling bride. Two chipped concrete steps led up to the front door, and two chipped concrete steps led out the back, trapping me as effectively as if it were the maximum security block at San Quentin. Were I somehow able to levitate myself and my chair out to the sidewalk, I could see miles of factories, warehouses, and seedy convenience groceries, which discouraged tourism.

The door opened onto a kitchen too small for me to turn my chair around in. Beyond was a living room the size of its couch and TV. To one side was the bedroom, which Muller had divided into two little cells separated by a screen, and a bathroom I never entered because the door was far too narrow.

In one of the sleeping cubicles was the main attraction: an ancient crank-operated hospital bed. Muller had been tending his seventy-year-old brother, a paraplegic, who had recently died of emaciation and bedsores. I often thought of him, lying where I now lay, on the same bed, under the same naked light bulb.

Getting out of bed, and set for the day, which I would spend parked in front of the kitchen breadboard, took three hours. Instead of a team of experts, one sixty-six-year-old retired machinist was available to wash me, see to the bowel program, get my catheter on right—if twisted, it swelled up like a water balloon and leaked—and get me dressed. At that time I had to wear brown hospital support stockings, a corset to help keep the blood from pooling in my stomach, and plaster wrist braces to keep my tendons from stretching. Rolling me back and forth, in the bed, Muller struggled with all this paraphernalia and exhausted himself. Finally, to get into the chair, I hung from a trapeze while he swung me over. Usually I landed wrong, pants all twisted and riding up into my crotch, white shins exposed. I learned years later to buy trousers one foot too long.

Right off the bat Muller started complaining about having to do the bowel program every day. "My brother Richard only shit once a week, fer Chrissake!" I tried to imagine what Muller had done with the results. Had them barged out to sea, perhaps? The thought surfaced that maybe Muller had stopped feeding Richard; but I repressed it.

There was no possibility of a real bath, since I couldn't get to the tub. I got a bed bath and I washed my hair—or tried to—in a pan placed on my lap. There was no way I could get it clean.

When my head itched, he would rub witch hazel into my scalp. "This'll help, fer Chrissake!"

Then Muller would worm my chair into the tiny kitchen and pull out the breadboard, which was my table. Conversation during this time generally revolved around Muller's sense of himself as an urbanite forced to deal with a hick. He had immigrated to the big city from Yuma, Arizona, sometime in the 1930s.

"What the fuck do you know, you're from the sticks! Now a man like me, I once saw *Clark Gable and Carole Lombard*, fer Chrissake!"

"Oh yeah? How are we holding out on beer?"

"Yer not listening, fer Chrissake!"

Finally, he would leave me alone to stare across the courtyard at the next apartment. I had no desire to read a book, to write, or to draw. A couple of times Muller lowered me down the steps so that I could sit in the sun for an hour. Nearly every day for six months I sat by the breadboard with my cigarettes, which he had to light for me, until it was time to go back to bed. This is going to be my life, I thought. Sitting, smoking, and trying to make conversation with an old redneck whose chief cultural interest is stock-car racing. I felt like Sylvia Plath's *The Hanging Man*:

> *A vulturous boredom*
> *Pinned me to this tree.*

Beyond the wall, on another breadboard every afternoon at precisely three o'clock, someone went chop chop chop, chopchop chopchopchopchopchopCHOPchopchop, cutting up fish for a family of newly immigrant Japanese.

The apartment on the other side was inhabited by at least a dozen Mexicans. *Their* sounds were screaming and wife beating.

Except for me, everybody in the complex who could speak English was over sixty, which put a damper on my social life.

In midafternoon, Al Muller would go shopping, leaving me alone with the third occupant of our home, his sixteen-year-old Yorkshire, Chopper.

You can never move in on an old dog. Chopper ignored all my attempts to make friends and gave total attention to his master. With Muller gone, he became very nervous. He would bark at anything, at atoms circulating in the air. If Muller was gone for two hours, that's how long Chopper barked. The sound reverberated off the bare walls and, along with the naked overhead bulbs, made me feel as if I were being softened up for questioning by the KGB.

Even with Muller at home, Chopper was always at the edge of canine paranoia. Once or twice a week the Arrowhead Water man delivered our drinking water to the porch at 6:00 A.M. (you don't drink the tap water in L.A.) and Chopper went absolutely berserk. He wanted to be young again, so that he could jump through the wall and bite the guy's head off. I love animals, but I used to pray for seven seconds during which I would stand up, walk across the room, and strangle Chopper by hand. Then I'd sit down, fulfilled and happy to be paralyzed for the rest of my life.

After a couple of hours with the dog, during which I couldn't light a cigarette, Muller would come back with a pint of vodka for himself, a six-pack of Coors for me, and Rice-A-Roni for both of us. Rice-A-Roni was Muller's favorite dish, so, just to simplify life, he cooked nothing else. One day he would add some hamburger, the next some tuna, and so forth. Can't we just once have Rice-A-Roni with pheasant under glass? I thought.

After dinner he moved me into the living room, my beer on my lap, and he sat on the couch with his dog and his screwdriver, and we watched TV. He always insisted on *Baretta*. "I went to the

same dentist as Robert Blake, fer Chrissake," he'd slur bitterly every night. At that time I didn't have the emotional or physical resources to wheel myself into the bedroom, to go off by myself and draw or read. So I sat with my jailer. I'd watch him sink lower and lower as the night wore on and so would I: I was still taking so much medication that a beer was the equivalent of a double martini. On the other hand, I couldn't get too drunk: I had to make sure Muller, who was after all a tired old man, got me into bed before he passed out himself. On the other hand, I couldn't get drunk enough: it took a whole six-pack to face the loneliness of that old bed under that bare bulb, that cell with the door left ajar in case I needed anything—provided, of course, that Muller was still functional enough to help me.

No amount of alcohol could help me with "pronation." To prevent bedsores I often had to sleep facedown, pillows lifting me just enough off the bed to breathe. Lacking the muscles to arch myself up, I was constantly on the edge of suffocation. On my back and with the bed cranked up, gravity was in my favor; pronated I couldn't move at all. To experience this for yourself, lie facedown and get a large man to stand between your shoulderblades while two others pin your arms. Stay like that for eight hours.

It was a big day for me when my folks sent me a little transistor radio so that I could listen to rock 'n' roll at night in bed. For the first couple of months at Al Muller's I had just watched planes going by through the little bedroom window.

Every week Al drove me back to Rancho for four hours of physical therapy. It was heaven compared to his apartment. One day, without telling him, I begged Fanny Gridley to get me out of there, and she arranged to transfer me to a nursing home. Muller flew into a rage when the van pulled up to take me away. I felt triumphant.

I lasted two days. The place smelled like the toilet in a bus station. I was in a three-bed room. On one side was a psychopathic black para, arms the size of your thigh and meaner than hell. On the other was a ninety-eight-year-old who communicated by blinking. The man in charge was a homosexual named Nightingale. After the second night I rolled myself down the hall to the pay phone and called Al Muller.

Muller gloated, and I was forced to grovel. To get even, I then hired an extremely snotty black teenager to drive me around the city once a week in a purple GTO. We'd cruise slowly through Watts while he explained the sights in a dialect that only occasionally sounded like English. Once, I mentioned that the traces of red polish on his nails seemed odd, and his answer came through clear as a bell:

"Not if you's a drag queen, Cal'han."

My family had pleaded with me to come back to Oregon after Rancho and I'd refused. I was going to make it or break it in L.A. Yet I found myself virtually locked up in a town where I knew no one and where I was isolated from everything, literally crying myself to sleep some nights, with nothing to look forward to but another day in Muller's four-by-four kitchen.

When, five months after my first introduction to Al Muller, my parents tried to persuade me again to move back to Oregon, I had very little resistance. My maternal grandmother lay dying in a nursing home administered by the Benedictine abbey at Mount Angel, Oregon. I could be a comfort to her. I let myself be shipped north.

MOUNT ANGEL ABBEY stood on the top of a hill in the lush Willamette Valley south of Portland, with a 360-degree view of its own hop fields. Monks always find the most beautiful place to build anything. Around a fifty-yard square were arranged brick classrooms and dormitories, chapels and the abbey church, and a world-famous library designed by Eero Saarinen. The abbey grew its own food. It milked its own cows. It had its own carpenters, plumbers, electricians, teachers, porn shops (just kidding!). It seemed as self-sufficient as anything in the Middle Ages.

The nursing home, in the nearby town of Mount Angel, was run by Benedictine sisters. They were tough and efficient, like my teachers at Saint Mary's Academy. So, as nursing homes go, it was outstanding; but it was still a place of death. The only persons not senile or terminally ill were myself and a Vietnam veteran about ten years older than me who was a spectacular amputee. He was also an alcoholic. His parents had talked him into moving to Mount Angel from the big VA Hospital in Portland, in the hope the nuns would control his drinking. We latched on to each other immediately.

Toby had been hit in the legs while on a long-range patrol and the only treatment he got for days was first aid. Later, osteomyelitis had set in, and his infected legs had had to be amputated, clear up to and including the hip joints. They fit what was left of him into a prosthesis called a "bucket," a fake set of hips and legs that sat in his wheelchair permanently dressed in corduroy pants, shoes, and socks.

Because of the extreme nature of his amputation Toby was prone to bedsores and could only sit in his bucket a couple of hours at a stretch; most of the time he had to pull himself around on a gurney. Nevertheless he joined me in raising as much hell as possible. I had the part-time loan of an electric wheelchair, and we played "Choo-choo Train": he'd hang on to the chair and I'd tow him and the gurney up and down the long corridors at top speed. The game ended when we swept around a corner one evening and totaled Sister Allison and her medication cart, which was loaded with everyone's bedtime dose of Valium and saltpeter. Toby slid off the gurney and landed on his back. He looked up at Sister Allison, who was trembling with rage, and remarked, "Sorry, Sister. My horse threw me."

The home was visited periodically by the Rebeccas, a Catholic women's service organization. There were always twenty or thirty extremely senile patients restrained in their wheelchairs in a row along the corridor near the nursing stations, and the Rebeccas, many of whom looked like candidates for the nursing home themselves, would pass along this line of vegetables shaking hands and dispensing cheer. Toby and I took up positions at the end of the line and joined in the handshaking, slobbering and drooling down our cheeks.

The nuns, who were RNs, quickly came to disapprove of us, once they found out how much we were drinking in our room. They tried to ban our liquor. But we had allies among the young student nurses. I was especially careful to cultivate the girls on the night shift, who had the keys to the icebox and could bring a snack for me (or, for that matter, be a snack for me).

Since I always had a few bucks from the insurance settlement I'd won after the accident, I could always get liquor. The janitor would be cleaning my room and I'd say, "Come on, Jake, why don't you take me downtown and I'll buy you lunch?" and we'd have lunch, after which I'd say, "Jake, just stop here at the liquor store for a moment, will you? I want to get a pint." Of course I couldn't pour for myself. If Toby wasn't around and I couldn't find one of our student-nurse friends, I had to sweet-talk an aide who didn't know about the house ban.

"Hey, Doreen, help me with this, will you? It's been a long day."

"Well . . . I don't know if I really should."

Later everyone wondered who Callahan had talked into helping him get drunk again. It wasn't long before Toby and I were called into the mother superior's office and told to shape up or ship out. It seemed advisable to move the scene of our debauches off campus.

In keeping with the general medieval theme of hierarchies, the town and its fleshpots lay below the abbey. Actually there was only one fleshpot, Tiny's Tavern, a huge barn of a place with real sawdust on the floor and no heat; in Tiny's either you were already drunk or you wore a coat. The place attracted farmhands, nursing-home patients and itinerant hippies. A good cross section of medieval-looking peasants.

Nearly every day we'd withdraw $40 from serious-faced Sister Rose in the business office, wheel down the hill, go to Tiny's, and get shit-faced. As the months went by, I was actually gaining motor skills: using a fixture on my splint, I could now raise a glass of the hard stuff to my lips.

Toby and I were quite a bizarre fixture in Tiny's. One type anybody in a wheelchair meets fairly frequently is the citizen who flatly disbelieves you're really crippled. To these guys it's all in the mind. One afternoon we were accosted by a Mount Angel college sophomore who had had a few and who was clearly affronted by the very sight of us. He came over and told us off.

"You guys are just fakers! If you really wanted to, you could use the power of your minds to get up out of those chairs and walk!"

"Yeah, I suppose you're right," agreed Toby. He put his hands down on his wheels and slowly lifted all that was left of his torso straight up out of his pants. With his elbows locked there were four inches of clear air above his belt buckle. The college kid's eyes bulged and he picked up his beer and just moved out, while the room full of regulars exploded with laughter.

Another regular at Tiny's was Brother Mark. Brother Mark was a young monk, about my age, highly cultured, articulate, and hopelessly alcoholic.

Brother Mark had Thursday afternoons off from three o'clock on, and we nearly always went out for a drink. Or for quite a few drinks. I was lucky to be in a wheelchair. Brother Mark had to be carried out to a cab on more than one occasion. He was always in trouble with the abbot. Besides being homosexual, he was on the plump side and wore heavy-rimmed glasses like Poindexter's, which made him look like the scholar he was and added comic effect when his face turned bright red and he screamed at somebody to step outside and duke it out. The evenings usually ended with him up on the table at Tiny's, holding up the skirts of his habit daintily to dance a jig while everybody in the place pounded out the time on the table with their beer mugs.

Sadly, Brother Mark lost his struggle to live by the Rule of Saint Benedict and left the order. Today he's a wino in Portland.

Among its enterprises, the abbey ran a seminary for the education of its priests and teaching brothers, with academic standards that would reduce the average American college student to a nervous wreck inside a week. Of course I was attracted to it. The mother superior spoke to the abbot. After a year of dealing with Callahan the Drunk, she was grasping at straws. I was allowed to take the entrance exam and somehow passed. I studied the English Romantic poets, Joyce, and Eliot. Years later I figured out that each class at the abbey cost me as much time and effort as five at Portland State University.

The interior of the abbey was like something out of James Joyce: severe-looking tonsured men in crisply ironed black robes, who had risen before dawn to sing matins, swept along freshly scoured marble corridors from this task to that. The place echoed with Gregorian chants, and the air carried the sharp scent of Lysol.

I always tried to be as inconspicuous as I could, parking my chair at the very back of each class of thirty monks, many of whom incongruously smoked cigarettes at their desks. But one morning suddenly I heard a dripping. My Texas catheter had sprung a leak! It sounded like a cow pissing on a flat rock. A brother had to be summoned with a bucket and mop to clean up the mess.

Even that embarrassment paled when, at the nursing home a few weeks later, student nurses giggled as they watched an RN nun trying to put the catheter on my dick. She had to give me a hard-on first. My mother never prepared me for things like this.

My increasingly dysfunctional urinary system began to give me agonizing headaches. One night I found myself in an ambulance speeding north the sixty miles to Portland for an ileal loop operation. At Good Samaritan Hospital, after about fifty preparatory enemas, surgeons constructed a new bladder from part of my intestine and attached a tube that runs from an orifice just to the right of and a little below my belly button directly into a urine bag. No more leaking catheters.

Pain knocked me flat for a few days, but as soon as I was able, I decided to test the new apparatus under field conditions. Right across the street from the recovery unit was a Portland landmark, the Lovejoy Tavern. A small bribe to the attendant cleared the way for me to sit in the Lovejoy all day knocking back double tequilas. I was now routinely drinking to blackout.

Back at Mount Angel, Toby and I continued to fight for sanity in the land of the dying. We weren't winning. At the end of one night's drinking we were crossing the railroad on our way home when Toby's manual wheelchair got stuck in the tracks. Struggling to get loose, he fell out of the chair. He lay across the tracks like the heroine in a Dudley Do-Right cartoon and moaned, "Go away, man. Leave me here. It's better this way." He wasn't kidding.

Somehow I talked him into holding on to my powered chair while I dragged him out of the right of way, and after a long struggle I freed up his wheels before the Midnight Special could flatten them.

Incidents like this led Sister Allison to tip off Alcoholics Anonymous, who sent a delegation to talk to us. They were a couple of older men in shapeless synthetic suits who looked like extras from *Night of the Living Dead*. I didn't relate to them. Besides, I didn't think I was an alcoholic. I did attend one AA meeting in Salem, the nearest sizable town; but that was just to keep the sisters happy so I could stay at Mount Angel.

Every day I would wheel my way down the hall to my grand-mother's room. She'd had a stroke and barely recognized me, but I held her hand and talked to her and tried to comfort her. Somehow her dying made me feel that my life was over too. I remembered a speech by Norman Bates, the crazed killer in Alfred Hitchcock's *Psycho:*

> Put her someplace? Have you seen the inside of one of those places? The laughter and the tears and the cruel eyes studying you?

The drinking got worse. The nuns on the night shift were furious when I showed up at the door at midnight, stinking, and had to be cleaned up and put into bed. Once, my foot fell off the pedal of my chair and dragged on the pavement all the way up the hill from Tiny's. Nobody noticed as the toe of my shoe wore through. Of course I couldn't feel it. By the time we reached the nursing home, all my toenails had been dragged off and I was gushing blood. This incident cost me a month in bed during which people smuggled booze in to me.

Finally at Oktoberfest, the town's beeriest celebration, the mother superior had me sign a secret agreement that I would not drink. Three days passed before I broke it, and was expelled.

I had been born to the nuns, schooled and nursed by them. Their peace, order and standards of excellence would always have a powerful attraction for me. "You fuckin' Catholics!" I yelled to Toby as they loaded me into the van. "I'm going to sign up with the Rastafarians!" But in truth I bitterly regretted my expulsion from the medieval calm of Mount Angel.

I MOVED TO the New Birth Nursing Home in Clackamas, a sub-
urb of Portland. I had my Mount Angel credits transferred to
Portland State University. New Birth, which cost me $1,300 a
month, was not up to nun standards. Typically there were ten girls
on shift for a patient population of four hundred dying old people stuck in an ugly, five-story brick eyesore. The staffers were all
eighteen-year-old three-hundred-pound chain-smokers named
Cheryl who had never finished kindergarten and spent most of
their time gossiping in the staff lounge.

A new one of these would appear each morning. "Hi, Mr. Callahan! I'm Cheryl. I'm here to get you up and off to school. You
need a bowel program this morning? Now tell me what to do.
We have fifteen minutes." God, I thought, no wonder I'm an alcoholic.

My roommates were nearly always in the last throes. More than
once I woke up in the morning and had to ring for the Cheryl on
duty.

"What do *you* want, Mr. Callahan," she'd ask, obviously put out.

"Well, my roommate here seems to be history. . . ." And sure
enough, the guy would be facedown in his breakfast tray when she
entered the room. "Must have been the powdered eggs," I'd grin.
They'd clean him up, and the undertakers would come and take
him away, making me even later for school.

Sometimes I'd sit staring out my window with a beer smuggled between my twenty-four-year-old knees feeling nauseous
with despair. My friends were all at college making something
of themselves. And here I sat, rotting. Was I being punished for
some bad thing I did? Was it my rebellion against the Church?
My doping? The trouble I had caused my parents? Or was it the
Ball Walk back at The Dalles drive-in?

I attended Portland State under the Vocational Rehabilitation Act, but I quickly muddied the water by letting myself be seduced by one of the school's handicapped services counselors. This might have been construed as a conflict of interest, but I was already conflicted and she, just separated from her husband, was very interested. It was fun, especially when we brought disabled-sex films to her apartment after work. We'd play them on the wall of her bedroom, have a good laugh, say, "No, no!" and then do whatever it was they were trying to demonstrate the correct way. When, finally, she told me I was "cut off," I had to ask, "From sex or from my funding?"

Although academically unchallenging, PSU was nerve-racking. In almost every class, we sat around in seminar-style circles, so everybody had a clear view when my leg spasmed and my shoe began to tap, tap taptapTAPTAPTAP on the pedal of my chair. I lived in dread fear of shitting in my pants due to the inadequate bowel programs I was getting or overflowing my pee bag because my drinking was totally out of control.

I sat in class feeling ragtag, unshaven, dirty, and sick from the previous night's cheap wine. Why the hell was I here with all these shiny little sophomores, all four or five years younger than me, with my urine bag exposed on the side of my wheelchair? By the time class was dismissed at 3:30 I felt drained, exhausted, eager to start the afternoon's drinking.

Not to worry, in a little while the Portland State lift bus would take me back across the river to the world of the dying, the restrained, the pissing-on-themselves. I studied—when I studied—with old people falling all over me. I loathed having some 112-year-old hag wander zombielike into my room, pick up my watch, and wander back out again while I watched helplessly from my bed.

On days when I didn't have to go to class, I would simply wheel myself down to the corner 7-Eleven and shell out a buck for a quart of white port. I would roll myself to a local park and sit there behind some trees, hoping no one could see me trying to twist open the screwtop with my shaking teeth. Then I would lift it to my mouth with both hands. I needed most of that first bottle just to get some relief.

Gradually other winos would drift into the park. I bought for them so that they would fetch my next quart. After a while I'd think, Hey, this is not so bad, even if I was sitting in my own shit, which was not unusual.

I spent eight months like that. Once, loaded, I fell forward out of my chair and broke my shoulder. Now I could mix pain pills with the booze. Almost daily I'd wake up out of a doze to find my arms spasming. I'd smell flesh burning and realize it was mine, that once again I had nodded out with a cigarette in my hand. I still have the scars.

Even the Cheryls started complaining. They didn't like being called "fucking cows" by a shitty cripple at 11:00 P.M. Every morning I climbed into my chair and set out on my Apology Route, begging forgiveness of anyone I thought I might have insulted in the previous night's blackout.

Somehow I continued to function in this condition. To get my coursework done, I rolled down to the lounge when all the old people were asleep. Always seeking the attention of women, I clowned, charmed, and tin-cupped my way to an average of three new dates a week on campus. Quite a few liked to hitch a ride from class to class on my lap. There was always some little girl willing to bring me a home-cooked meal or sneak in through a window after-hours. And every two months or so, my family visited.

But these seemed like the last favors accorded a condemned prisoner. I sensed that if I stayed at New Birth I'd be cold meat before long. So in the summer of 1976 I put an ad in the newsletter of the Spinal Cord Injury Association and began interviewing prospective attendants.

One day, a bisexual named Arnie came into the nursing home looking for the job. At first he reminded me of Brother Mark. We seemed to hit it off, so I gave Arnie a couple of thousand dollars and told him to go find us an apartment and fix it up.

Arnie rented us a two-bedroom, ground-floor apartment on a cul-de-sac in a pleasant section of southwest Portland, right against a wooded park. He packed my bags and loaded them and me into the van I'd purchased with settlement money but, up to now, rarely used since it wasn't equipped with quad controls. I hadn't had a place of my own since leaving The Dalles five years earlier, so this was a moment worth celebrating.

We stopped at the liquor store. For me, a fifth of Seagram's 7. For Arnie, a fifth of 100-proof Southern Comfort, the syrupy hooch that polished off Janis Joplin.

Most of our furniture hadn't yet been delivered, so we sat in the bare living room and emptied both bottles, joking and laughing hilariously. Presently Arnie excused himself.

Strange noises then came from the bathroom. "WUFF. WUFFF. HONK. HONK. HOOOONK!" Arnie returned, his eyes watering.

"For Chrissake, Arnie, that sounded like a goose being raped by a lesbian Hell's Angel. What gives?"

"It's none of your business, but I have a small sinus problem. I'd appreciate it if you didn't refer to it again."

As it turned out, Arnie consumed more nose medicine than Felix in *The Odd Couple*. Also like Felix, he was a neat freak. When he wasn't in the bathroom mixing up strange brews of Sinex, Coricidin and Anahist, or primping, he cleaned. I would wake up in the morning and hear, *Pssssss. Pssssss. Pssssss. Pssssss.* Arnie would be in the hall outside the apartment spraying the walls and baseboards with Lysol and Glade. He would have vacuumed the sidewalk, only being in public made him self-conscious. His mother must have given him a wastebasket on his third birthday.

Arnie's anal compulsions were exaggerated by the fact that he was a failure sexually. He was a sociopath. On his night off he would go out to the bars and fail to meet anybody male *or* female. This was in 1976, long before AIDS, when gay men were setting records for casual sex that will probably stand forever. But Arnie was missing it all.

As a result he was insanely jealous of my social life, even though I was only a straight. If I had somebody over, he made the worst of it. I remember one evening when I had a date with Stephanie, a teacher for the deaf. We were watching TV and eating Chee-tos in the front room. Arnie got the vacuum cleaner out and started vacuuming between Stephanie's feet, just to let her know that there was no invading his kingdom.

I had begun to enjoy a small circle of friends, some from school, some old pals from The Dalles who had moved to Portland. They felt uncomfortable at my apartment. I began to feel uncomfortable when they were there. After a while I stopped inviting family and friends over. I lived in dread fear of offending Arnie. I thought I would end up back in the nursing home.

I tried to cope with him in various ways. I introduced him to a gay friend of mine who also had sinus trouble. But Arnie rejected kinship. "I have sinus *problems.* I wouldn't say I have sinus *trouble.*"

Once I suggested, "Arnie, why don't you just go straight and get a girlfriend?" He said, "You know, I like making love to a girl. But it's so *messy.*"

Trapped with each other, we often ended the evening with a

drunken fight. He had a pronounced mean streak. One night I was lying naked in bed, we were halfway through my pre-bedtime program. In a rage Arnie picked up the half-gallon urinal into which he had just emptied my bag and poured piss all over my face. Then he stomped out.

I spent the night lying in my own piss without any covers, freezing.

Arnie frequently ended our fights by leaving me high and dry for hours at a stretch. I would be set up with a pitcher full of booze and 7-Up, a tube taped to it so that I could drink while he was gone all day. He used to leave a burning candle at my bedside so that I could light cigarettes. Needless to say a quadriplegic should not smoke or have an open flame around when alone. Once I dropped a burning cigarette behind me on the bed. Fortunately Arnie came home minutes later and saved the day.

Installment payments were coming in from my settlement, so I gave Arnie another thousand dollars and had him buy two color TVs. Now he could drink in front of his TV in the front room and I could stay in bed all day and all night with mine. I hated Arnie's guts at that time, but in fact I was isolating myself, Arnie or no Arnie. I got up only to go to my seventy-dollars-once-a-week psychiatrist, where I learned that I regarded my attendants as jailers.

In the psychiatrist's office I did battle with the circular reasoning that kept me prisoner in my own alcoholic mind. I had horrible panic attacks as I felt him penetrate my defenses, which, of course, was what I was paying him to do. After each session I had to hide in my bed, shades drawn. I had Arnie unplug the phone and stand guard against visitors while I healed.

Arnie, to give the devil his due, was a terrific cook, who never made beef stew when *boeuf bourguignon* would do. Once he spent all day laboring over a huge pot of navy beans and ham hocks and ended by dropping the tray, spilling everything. He sat down next to the mess, in such anguish that he couldn't even clean, and wept like Judas.

Nevertheless it was a great relief when I found someone else who met my minimum employment requirements: you had to be a fellow alcoholic willing to work terrible hours at unsavory tasks for almost nothing. Alex was my age and usually drunk *and* stoned. With him he brought several cats—and an epidemic of fleas. For some reason I was immune; but my mental picture of Alex in those days is of a slim, tall, mustachioed young man with a joint in one hand, a beer in the other, jumping from the bites of the fleas that swarmed in his chest hair. He was also a manic depressive on a maintenance diet of lithium, and a great killer of possums.

Portland, Oregon, is situated at the confluence of the Columbia and Willamette rivers. Much of it sits on what used to be a marshy floodplain before the great dams were built, starting in the 1930s. There are still dozens of channels and canals and thousands of drainage ditches. This urban wetland breeds uncounted possums, huge gray rodents with red eyes who scurry about at night in search of garbage. They furnish great sport for the citizenry. Even though it's illegal to discharge firearms within the city limits, many are taken each year with shotguns and .22s. But the classic way to hunt possums in Portland is with an automobile.

Alex was a master possum driver. The secret of his success was that he was absolutely relentless. I rode in the back of the van with my chair strapped down while Alex drove. We helled all over town, went to the coast, hosted van parties. One night we picked up an attractive young woman hitchhiker. We were driving through the northwest industrial district, an especially wet zone, when suddenly Alex spied a big one crossing the road up ahead. A three-footer! Instantly he downshifted and put the pedal to the metal, but the possum dove into a ditch.

Alex didn't hesitate: he followed the possum into the ditch at fifty miles per hour. The girl screamed and my head bounced off the ceiling. Alex swerved up out of the ditch, screeched to a halt, and looked back. In the dim red glow of the taillights we could just make out the badly injured animal limping back across the road. Alex slammed into reverse and nearly blew up the engine getting back to that possum to hit it again and put it out of its misery. He was a true sportsman. The girl, on the other hand, asked to be let out at the next light. She must have been sure she had wandered into a Truman Capote novel.

All that winter and into the spring I lost ground to booze. I was now drinking a maintenance fifth, usually of tequila, plus "social" drinks amounting to another fifth. Gradually I stopped going out and just drank my two fifths at home. I avoided situations where being drunk would seem inappropriate and I avoided people who weren't also drunks—99 percent of the real world, as it was. Isolating myself made it much easier to deny that I had a drinking problem.

But now I began to have withdrawal symptoms. I woke up each morning in a cold sweat. A terrible paranoia swept over me as dawn broke. I felt myself on the verge of hallucinations that never quite came. I felt terrified that I might be going insane.

So, I would try to ride through the day without a drink. I drew the shades, but it was still too light. I made Alex cover the windows with blankets. Light made the fear so much worse. I had to be in the dark.

"Move the TV in a little closer," I told him. I stared and stared at the tube, trying to focus my mind so that it wouldn't think about going crazy. But it would immediately start drifting off into, "I'm scared, I'm scared."

That ambulance! Was it taking away someone who'd gone crazy, like me? I knew I was going to end up chained in a nut-house.

I hated any noise. I hated Alex coming close to talk to me because he might see that I was going crazy. I couldn't stand the itching that spread over my whole body in waves, and I couldn't satisfy it by scratching.

I'd make it to three o'clock. To ten. If I made it to midnight or one o'clock, I'd begin to feel better, to feel sleepy, to fall into a couple of hours of light sleep, then a period of waking, then a couple more before I was fully awake in the predawn, waiting for the sunrise.

I didn't think I had a drinking problem. I attributed my symptoms to the effects of alcohol on quadriplegia. That let me off the hook.

I'd last up to three days before having that one little innocent drink.

It was always for a good reason, never because I was addicted to the stuff.

Once, I stayed drunk for an entire week; there was no paranoia that way. But when I came off it, I had the fear so bad that I stayed in the bathtub for three hours, shaking and crying and gulping Valium after Valium. At the end of it I didn't dare drink more than one day at a time, so the pattern became a dry day, followed by a drunk, followed by another nervous dry day, and so on.

Finally, on June 22, 1978, Alex woke me and left to do some errands. He put a bottle within reach, but I forgot to ask him to open it.

The damn thing had a tight cork. I clamped the bottle as tightly as I could between my hands and tore at the cork with my teeth, which were permanently chipped from having opened hundreds of screwtops and corks in the six years since my hands had last been able to perform such tasks. I twisted and chewed at it for an hour, the sweat streaming down my face and blurring my eyes.

When I dropped the bottle, watching it roll away across the rug, something snapped. Alex would be gone all day. There was nothing I could do. For what must have been hours I stared at the bottle on the floor, rage building inside me.

I began to scream. I screamed at God. "You son of a bitch! You got me into this! You're responsible for my life! You put me in this situation! Bastard! Shithead!" and on and on until my voice was gone and my energy completely drained.

I exhausted myself. I began to break down. I began to cry like a kid. It was as if something was crying through me rather than me doing it. All my life, my childhood, my lost mother, the old people dying, Kurt, my useless body flowed through the tears. I cried for an hour straight.

And then I felt—and it was not a mental image but an actual

physical sensation—a hand begin to pat me on my back. A real hand, comforting me; but I knew as I looked to find it that it wouldn't be there.

Something was changing in me. Something had said, "This guy's had enough suffering, I'm gonna take it away from him."

When I rolled my chair over to the phone and dialed the number I had long known I would someday call, it was not a decisive act but merely the consequence of something that had already happened. I knew with utter certainty that my problem was not quadriplegia, it was alcoholism; that I was powerless to do anything about it by myself; and that I would never drink again.

CHAPTER 6

When Alex came back from shopping, my face was still tight with dried tears. "Hey, Alex, something really profound happened to me here. I don't think I'm gonna drink anymore."

"Yeah? Great. Uh, can I have some of these cookies?"

Oblivious, Alex proceeded to deal with a pot smoker's blood-sugar crisis. There was really no reason why he should have believed what I had just told him. In the past, whenever I'd had a particularly good session with my psychiatrist, we had celebrated by going out for a drink.

On the other hand, the psychiatrist, who had been working toward this goal for some time, was delighted. Only a week or so before, he had suddenly remarked, "You know, John, we have to make a decision here: whether you are going to be an inpatient or an outpatient."

He was talking about treatment for alcoholism. Whatever had given him the idea that I was an alcoholic?

Now he signed me up for a federally supported outpatient program. I was to attend two private sessions plus one group session each week. Later, when he felt I was up to it, I would start attending meetings of Alcoholics Anonymous. And, if I wanted to survive, he suggested I remain a member of that fellowship for the rest of my life. Despite the TV ads for private clinics, alcoholism isn't something that could be cured in "just ten days and a couple of follow-ups."

I took my first drink when I was thirteen. Thereafter, every time I encountered emotional stress, I took another, and I continued literally "feeling no pain" for much of the next fourteen years. Feeling no pain meant never having to learn to cope with it. All the normal "growing pains" of adolescence and young manhood passed me by. I was now twenty-seven, but emotionally I was still a child.

What I *had* learned, and learned thoroughly, was how to lie with a straight face, how to please people in order to manipulate them, how to deny responsibility, how to pass guilt along to others, and to be a law unto myself. Success at these things was constantly reinforced: if I did them well, I got to go on drinking. And so long as I was drunk, I didn't have to pass judgment on myself or notice the damage I was doing to the people around me.

The federal counselor turned out to be a leather-skinned ex-factory worker, sober maybe two years, who had taken a short course in counseling. A nuts-and-bolts kind of guy, he was still compulsive: he chain-smoked and drank coffee continuously. He gave me a primer on the disease, which I read and reread, and he gave me plenty of helpful hints: what foods to eat, how many glasses of water to drink, how an occasional tablespoonful of honey helped the body to withdraw from a booze diet that might as well have consisted of twenty-two Mars bars a day, so far as blood sugar was concerned.

In the federal program's group sessions, everybody was a beginner, and all nerves were on edge. "John doesn't seem to be talking much in this group. Maybe he thinks he's better than the rest of us."

I thought, I sure do, you retarded white-trash buttfucker.

My irritability, when I stopped drinking—and smoking, too, at the same time—began to alternate with an acute nervous sensitivity.

For weeks I felt exhausted. I longed for sleep. But somebody always seemed to be watching TV in the living room. The refrigerator never stopped humming away in the kitchen. There was a jackhammer outside, a baby crying across the hall, a fly buzzing around my head. I couldn't find a way to turn down the noise. Even lights were irritating to me.

This state of mind was with me twenty-four hours a day. It even seemed to pursue me into my dreams. Awake, I often felt as if I'd had an entire layer of skin removed. The Flayed Man.

I had always been a worrywart and had gotten much worse after the accident. But now I developed a positive *need* to worry. That Alex wouldn't pick me up on time. That my pee bag would leak. That I smelled bad. That the store would be out of orange juice. That if they had it, it would be laced with cyanide. That the sun wouldn't come up. That I wasn't really paralyzed.

In the car I was sure we were going to have an accident (not really a neurotic worry, since Alex habitually drove with a joint in his hand and an open can of beer clamped between his thighs). I began to avoid the group meetings with their unpleasant encounters that triggered my anger. I committed small acts of rebellion against my counselor. "How can I help you when you won't even fill out the goddamn forms!" he roared at me.

"You know, John," he remarked one day, "I regard your friend there as wearing the black hat in this situation." From his office he had a view of Alex, waiting in the parking lot with joint in hand and beer on lap.

It was true that our relationship was becoming strained, but it was not just Alex's doping and drinking. Sober, I had to come to terms with my paralysis all over again. I had never really faced my helplessness. It drove me crazy to see Alex exercising my legs, which I couldn't feel, or getting my pants on crooked, as usual:

"Uh, do you suppose you could scoot them down a little? I'm having trouble speaking through the fly."

"If I feel like it, fuckface," he'd offer, nursing his daily hangover.

I soon couldn't bear to have him touch me. I refused to be touched on that unfeeling skin.

I felt raw fear, the fear of not getting my needs met. It was rooted in my abandonment by my real mother at birth and exacerbated tenfold by the paralysis. For three hours every day my body was penetrated, pumped out, squeezed dry, scrubbed down, hoisted up and down and dressed to the standards of a baggy-pants comedian. Every day, as it would be forever. Most of the time I was having my very pimples popped by guys I couldn't really relate to, misfits and oddballs who were all I could afford. Even the occasional friendship was soured by dependence. Sometimes all I wanted to say to Alex was, "Straighten my pants out, you stupid fucking lackey! Straighten them, you bastard!" Of course I couldn't. Alex was not just my attendant, he was my buddy.

When something did snap and I screamed at Alex, he would stomp out and leave me high and dry for an hour. After such a confrontation I felt hung over from the adrenaline and emotional turmoil. When I arrived at school, I'd sometimes sit alone and try to pull myself together, feeling horribly guilty about losing my control with Alex. But he stayed with me. I think he understood.

Sometimes, in the warmth of the summer sun, I'd sit in the blackberry patch behind our apartment and close my eyes. All would be still for a moment. I felt relieved, and able to derive some pleasure from the same acute sensitivity that had been driving me insane. I felt I was being healed by an outside power, a sensation I'd heard reported by other newly sober people.

But in bed alone at night I knew that I had no control whatever. I was sure that my life was going to accelerate downward into chaos and misery. It always had.

In my eagerness to clean myself out, I decided to stop taking a mild mood-elevating drug prescribed by my psychiatrist. The federal counselor found out and flew into a rage. He made me agree to take the pills again; but I gave myself half-doses and rapidly tapered off. After that the closest thing to a drug I used was herbal tea.

I began to read the Big Book—the bible of Alcoholics Anonymous. From the moment I opened it, I knew instinctively that the program it described was for me. I went along with Alex to his work as a gardener, and while he tended shrubs, I sat in the sun with my book. At home I kept it on my lap while I rolled constantly from room to room to build up my strength; in the end I virtually memorized it. My first act after I hit bottom had been to call the AA hotline, but the federal counselor had discouraged me from going to a meeting. He felt I wasn't ready yet for that much reality.

After nine years of continuous sobriety, it's my considered opinion that any alcoholic who expresses the slightest desire to go to a meeting of this fellowship should be put into a Life Flight helicopter, or whatever vehicle is fastest, and taken there at once.

In my raw state I was terrified of facing one of these meetings. But I couldn't endure many more of these nights either.

I tried my best to exhaust myself before putting out the light, knowing what I was in for, but sleep never came in time to save me. Instead my mind began to search itself, and I would start to feel the cold, a cold all the way down to my very soul. This awful ache. This horrible, hollow, lonely, gnawing, freezing emptiness inside. My whole being seemed to stretch out into the universe in this frozen ache.

A friend had given me a subscription to a nonsectarian pamphlet of meditations, *The Daily Word*. Once I would have regarded such a thing as ludicrously irrelevant to my life, but not now. From it I learned an exercise called "Flight of the Pelican," in which I imagined myself as the huge bird, reaching for the sky, gathering more and more momentum with each thrust of my powerful wings. That was one alternative to a scream of despair.

I used to rock myself, as much as a paralytic can rock himself. I would pull the sheets up over my eyes and shake my head back and forth, back and forth, to warm and comfort myself. I wanted to cry out for help, but to whom, or to what? If I felt like this, there could be no God.

My counselor tried to reassure me. "You're right on schedule," he'd say. But I felt I was turning into some morbidly hypersensitive lunatic out of a tale by Edgar Allan Poe.

Often I felt that nothing was working. Even today there are periods when I feel fallen apart, emotionally and physically. This happens generally in the wintertime, on a weekend, around the holidays. The cushion on my chair will be wrong. The foot pedals will be wrong. I'll be sitting crookedly. My pants will be twisted and too low and digging into my stomach. But I can't stop some stranger on the street and say, "Would you undo my pants and straighten them up around my waist?"

Some days when I ventured out alone in my chair, I'd see myself mirrored in the window of some store and I'd look really bad. I'd be dressed in all the wrong clothes. But there was no whipping on home and doing a quick change. Sometimes I did go home . . . but only to hide for the rest of the day in my apartment.

Sometimes, when trying to get in, I'd drop my keys. Then I would sit in the 32-degree cold, waiting for some tenant to wander by and let me in.

I fantasized making a pact with the Devil for a day off. I'd jump into my jeans, fly to San Francisco and be anonymous for the day, finish up with dinner at the Blue Fox with an expensive call girl. Hopefully nobody would spot me. "Hey, you're supposed to be a quad! What the hell is going on?" Then I'd fly back to Portland, jump into bed and lose the feeling in my legs.

After a month of sobriety I finally decided to go to an AA meeting, ready or not. Alex lowered me down the steps of a church basement, the first of many. The crowd was from an affluent part of town; stockbrokers and well-dressed wives gathered around a huge coffeepot like votives at a shrine.

I didn't exactly blend in. Everybody in the room turned to look at this neon cripple from outer space. I fought an urge to have Alex haul me back up the steps. I felt sure somebody would come over and say, "Sorry. We can't have anyone this grotesque in here."

The meeting began with a moment of silence followed by Saint Francis of Asissi's famous prayer:

God, grant me the serenity
To accept the things I cannot change;
The courage to change the things I can
And the wisdom to know the difference.

Tradition required that the leader ask if anybody present was at his first meeting of the fellowship or in his first thirty days of continuous sobriety. My response was supposed to be, "My name is John, and I'm an alcoholic." Everyone then would look at me and chant in unison, "Hi, John! Welcome!" After a couple of times this began to drive me nuts. It's one good reason not to drink; if you fall off the wagon, you have to endure thirty more days of this greeting.

At the time, ignorant of the ritual and exploding with tension, I didn't wait to be introduced. I blurted out, "I was paralyzed in a car accident in 1972." I still cringe when I recall this moment.

The first part of the meeting could have been the sabbath of some minor sect. The Twelve Steps of the AA program and its traditions were read aloud by some of the members, followed by a passage from a book of daily meditations. Then the chairperson, an old-timer, read a quote from the Big Book, put it down, and began to talk.

"When I got into this program, I had two pairs of pants. One with shit in them and one without. And I didn't much care which of them I was wearing. . . ."

Suddenly he had my total attention. Was this old character reading my diary?

For most of the next hour anyone who felt like "sharing" could take the floor. Some of the statements were merely testimonials to the effectiveness of the program, but many others offered the most intimate sort of revelations. People vented their anger, whined and complained, boasted, told how scared they were, reported victories in their lives, recounted failures, and in general offered help and support to one another. At the end everybody joined hands, recited the Lord's Prayer, and then shouted, "Keep coming back! It works!"

Beginners were supposed to try to attend at least one meeting every day for ninety days. Terminally self-conscious, I was terrified in each and every one of mine. My palms, though I couldn't feel them, were sweating. I was scared that a bowel or bladder accident would force me to need to leave the room. I dreaded the passing of the collection basket because people would be able to see how little strength I had in my hands. I cringed at the condescension I sometimes had to endure:

"Christ, I thought *I* had it bad! There's some poor bastard back there in a goddamn wheelchair! I'll bet he has a story. . . ."

Most of all I was afraid I was going to be asked to speak in a meeting. The mere thought of doing so gave me a panic attack. "If you're so fucking nervous in those meetings," Alex would snap, "just don't go to them." But I no longer had a choice. The fellowship and its program were my last hope.

Every meeting was different, but there were certain constants. Signs pinned up on the walls: "Easy Does It"; "Live and Let Live"; "I Am Responsible"; "One Day at a Time"; "Exit". A blue haze of cigarette smoke and the omnipresent big institutional coffee urn. Once I got over my initial distrust of the members, I began to notice their honesty. People were either telling the truth or trying to. I was told that if I continued to go to meetings, I would sooner or later hear some stranger tell my story. One night I went to a candlelight meeting with my new buddy Heavy Metal Mike, who is still my closest AA friend. The crowd was young, and there in the darkness I heard a girl tell part of mine:

"I was down on my hands and knees in the bathroom. I had to take my pills but I was nauseous. I vomited them back up. But I felt I had to take them so I ate them with the vomit from my hand. I looked up at the ceiling, and I said, 'God, why do I have to do this?'"

When she got done, the roomful of drunks was sniffling.

Old-timers in the program urged me to waste no time in finding a sponsor, an experienced recovering alcoholic who would serve as my guide through the Twelve Steps, designed not just to free me from the need to drink but to repair my character defects and to give me a set of tools with which to live my life. After a few weeks of meetings I heard a speaker say, "I haven't had a drink, now, for seven years. But tomorrow morning I'm going to start the day with a beer!" This remark set the room abuzz. It was a shocking and effective way to make the point that an alcoholic is never cured and must always live "one day at a time." I liked this guy's approach and decided to get to know him better. So, after the meeting, I rolled up to him. "Hi, I'm John. I really liked what you had to say. Have you got a few minutes?"

Donny was thirty-six, nine years older than me. He was a millionaire, having inherited the fortune his parents had made in the antique business, but he always worked. When I met him, he had just begun teaching English in a Catholic school. As he drove around, he played Chaucer tapes on his car stereo. He was an active homosexual, which gave him an "outsider's" viewpoint, something with which I could identify. He seemed absolutely confident, always friendly but firm about what I must do. "Go to the meetings. Read the book. Don't drink." I came to rely on him as a child relies on his father.

The program's First Step, to admit that I was powerless over alcohol and that my life had become unmanageable, was easy. A paralyzed alcoholic gets a double dose of powerlessness. Every morning when my attendant shoved a gloved finger up my rectum, every time the seal of my urine bag leaked at a social event, every time I spent a day in bed because my chair had a flat tire, I was reminded in the most rudimentary way of my powerlessness.

Not that I was entirely helpless. The nuns and the monks had left their mark on me; I knew I was capable of hard intellectual work. My real parents, whoever they were, had left me with a creative instinct that had persisted, in spite of everything, since childhood.

But I had to face the fact that my best thinking thus far had brought me to the doors of this fellowship suicidal and pissing on myself. I hadn't scored any victories over alcoholism, the disease that insists, "You have no disease." I had merely stretched my rationale until it snapped. And I had no more idea how to live than does a newborn babe.

The Second Step was not so easy. It asked me to come to believe that a Power greater than myself could restore me to sanity.

I was, as many alcoholics say jokingly, a "recovering Catholic." I choked on the word *God*. To me it implied a remote, implacable, white-bearded father figure who handed out intergalactic brownie points through cadres of black-robed bureaucrats. One wasn't supposed to question why he allowed millions to starve or die in miserable wars.

But on the day I had stopped drinking, I had had a direct experience that shook my disbelief and undermined my intellectual pride. Now I was at least *willing* to *come* to believe that some sort of Power might be able to restore me to sanity.

The program emphatically stated that I didn't have to choose any particular Higher Power. It didn't have to be Jesus, or Buddha, or Vanna White. If I had wanted to, I could have chosen a doorknob, or Alex's beard (I was counseled against choosing the genitalia of Raquel Welch by my sponsor). Donny, who always called his Higher Power Chuckie, taught me that the important thing was to start thinking about something outside yourself for a change, to recognize in some token way that you are not running the universe and that it would very likely continue in your absence. You can't ask for help if you don't think there's anybody to give it.

But I was advised not to linger too long over the question of belief. The important thing was to jump in and get to work, to "trust in God and clean house."

Donny and I were both attracted to Eastern thought. We read Lao-tzu together, and I was delighted by the practical, down-to-earth quality of his teaching. "It's the void in the middle of the vase that makes it valuable," he wrote. That spoke to the sense of loss that was at the center of my own life.

AA took a very broad view of spirituality. It had been founded, in the 1930s, by a surgeon and a stockbroker and about a hundred other ordinary drunks who discovered that by working with each other they could stay sober. Like many of them, I was hungry for tools and impatient with religious hocus-pocus. Once, ready to try anything, I made an appointment to see an Indian guru over on the other side of town. Heavy Metal Mike drove me over. The guru came out and we talked for a while. He said, "Listen, my son. You are fortunate."

"What do you mean?"

"You are in an excellent position for spiritual growth."

Fuck spiritual growth, I thought. I wanted to feel my own body, jump around, and be free of these crazy attendants.

Step Three required me to make a decision to turn my will and my life over to the care of God *as I understood him.* But I had been indoctrinated with the Catholic idea of God, which I hated. How in the world, I thought, can I make such a decision? I decided to settle for being *willing* to make such a decision. God could come later.

Donny and I went out to the sunny blackberry patch behind my house and I made a short prayer, and with as much earnestness as I could summon I took Step Three.

Even to get this far was hard work. All through my first weeks in the program I remained prey to violent mood swings; my physical limitations frustrated me terribly. I'd reach for the phone and drop it. In my attempts to pick it back up, I'd knock over the fishbowl; as I fled across the room from the site of this humiliation, I'd hear the phone clanging along behind me. The cord would have gotten caught up in my wheels (things like this still happen to me). Once I smashed every dish in the house, literally, out of rage. I hated my body so much I would smash my hand against the wall and scream. It's a miracle I never broke a bone.

AA has a phrase, "Sit still and hurt." It means, Don't run away from your feelings. I'd been sitting still, all right, but running far and fast from my feelings.

Once a week I spent a day in bed. I can remember looking at my body with loathing and thinking, Boy, if I ever get to heaven, I'm not going to ask for a new pair of legs like the average quad does. I'm going to ask for a dick I can feel. The idea promoted in rehab of the socially well-adjusted, happily married quad made me sick.

This was the cruelest thing of all. Always, I felt humiliated. Surely a man with any self-respect would pull the plug on himself. Razor blades were one obvious choice. Or I could hang myself from one of the straps on my bed's overhead frame. I could set the chair in reverse and just let it back out from under me. Years later

I drew a cartoon about that moment. It pictures a centaur with his human part dressed as a cowboy. He's decided to end it all. He's got a noose around his neck and the rope over the limb of a tree, and he's hitting himself on the rump with his Stetson to spook himself into a gallop. At the time, though, I didn't have a joke left in me. My face wet with tears of bitterness and despair, I thought, If you're not there God, I'm fucked.

But there was a telephone next to my bed, and my sponsor was always at the other end of the line. I could call up at 3:00 A.M. and say, "Donny, I can't move my legs. I'm going crazy."

He'd always say, "What are the first Three Steps?" And I'd have to recite them. Then he'd say, "Well, since you admit that you're powerless over your quadriplegia and believe that a Higher Power than yourself can restore you to sanity, wouldn't you like to turn this over to Chuckie?" And I'd once again make a decision to turn my will and my life over to the care of Chuckie where quadriplegia was concerned.

Donny was patient with me. I was asked several times to chair a meeting. But I had a terrible fear of speaking, or even appearing in front of large numbers of people. I remembered my high school graduation in a huge gymnasium filled with hundreds of people. I had marched in with Foley's sister, both of us in blue satin caps and gowns, and I guided us, instinctively, to the back row of the section reserved for the seniors. I'd had a few hits from a bottle with the guys out on the playground. But as I sat there listening to the keynote speaker, imagining hundreds of eyes staring at me, I suddenly felt a terrible panic rise up, and I got up, with the excuse that I was going to the john, and walked out, in front of the whole crowd. I didn't come back. They found me out on the playground later—Foley's sister had to suffer the embarrassment of marching out alone. The family had come from all over the state to see me graduate and my father was furious. "You're a goddamn coward!" he said. I hated him for saying it; it was just what I was thinking myself.

But when I couldn't chair the AA meeting and I turned to Donny with tears of frustration, saying, "I wanted to do it, I wanted to do it!" he just patted me on the shoulder and said, "Next time."

Another thing he did was to set up what he called a God Basket. He taped a medium-size brown paper shopping bag to the wall up near the ceiling like a little basketball hoop. He wrote "Chuckie" on it. When I had a problem, I'd write, for example, on a piece of paper: "I am worried about the rent. I don't have the money! Who is going to pay the fucking rent?" I'd fold the paper up, and my attendant would toss it into the God Basket. Thus I acknowledged my powerlessness over things I could do nothing about and got rid of the frustration and the sense of injustice they engendered.

According to AA, self-pity was "like wetting your pants in the winter, a very warm feeling for a very short time." I fought the feeling that I had a legitimate *case* for self-pity. There was nobody in the fellowship in a wheelchair at that time who could bust me down, who could say, "Listen, fuckface, I'm in a wheelchair too. How are you gonna take *me* on?" I told Donny that what I really needed was to be in a special group for handicapped alcoholics, because we had special problems.

He said, "Yeah, they could call it the Self-pity Group."

So I simply relied on the authority of the program itself, which said that self-pity would lead me back to the bottle: "Poor me, poor me, pour me a drink."

For a while I attended the meetings of a real hard-core group dominated by old-timers who could have passed for Zen masters. Reba was an old Irishwoman who used to chair some of the meetings. She was broad-shouldered, with owl glasses, a tiny pert mouth, and alert eyes, which darted back and forth. She reminded me of an old nun.

"When I first came to these meetings," she frequently told us, "I was a *big, fat, worthless cow!* I worked these steps and I *carved* a life for myself."

Jesus Christ, I thought, there's something about this woman! She had the finesse of a drill sergeant. "This is the Scolley Group and we do not chat across the table in the Scolley Group, because some of us have incurred brain damage through our drinking and our *attention spans are short!*"

I imagined that she would take me out behind the woodshed and flog me to death with a switch on my nonfeeling buttocks if I broke the rule. Actually I got along fine with Reba, but she didn't like Alex, who used to complain to her that he wanted to stop drinking but couldn't. "It takes what it takes, my fine-feathered friend," was all she would say.

Reba died of cancer of the heart five years later in the fall of 1983. I visited her regularly, and she became sweeter and sweeter as death approached. Her legacy to me included many tools, not the least of which was this thought:

"There's nobody too stupid for this program, but there are a lot of people too damn smart for it."

All those weeks Alex must have felt like a demon present at an exorcism. Many of my meetings took place in a big converted mansion that had been remodeled into a clubhouse. There was no wheelchair access at that time. Alex, with the help of whoever was present, had to drag me up the steps. Once inside, I was on a main floor devoted to lounges and a coffee shop. The meeting rooms were either up one big flight of stairs or down another. When he had muscled me into the room, Alex usually took off. But sometimes he stayed for the solid hour of testimonials, bellyaching, and prayer. If the chairperson made the mistake of closing the meeting by asking, "Does anyone have anything else to say before we join hands for the Lord's Prayer?" Alex would raise his hand and get in his two bits worth.

"Well, now, I think you boys are being a little heavy-handed and obsessive about all this. I think just a *moderate* amount of churchgoing . . ." And the old-timers would begin to cough and shuffle their feet.

I made Alex nail up favorite sayings or slogans on my walls. Being reminded of them took the edge off my constant anxiety. To put "Thy Will Be Done" over the kitchen stove, he had to climb above the level of ambient pot smoke, which must have seemed frightening. When I got on his case about all the pot, he'd snap back, "Well *of course* I'm stoned!"

Alex's addictions were threatening my recovery, and I knew I had to replace him. The fear of a new attendant was—and is— massive. Imagine that you are going to be utterly dependent on some weirdo for months. That you are going to submit to a repugnant intimacy with him several hours a day. That if he is five minutes late, you are going to look out the window and feel certain that your whole day has just been ruined because he's quit, he's sick, he's had a car wreck, he's been murdered by terrorists. Forget getting out of bed. Forget breakfast. The most you can do is pick up the telephone.

At this time my normal, everyday anxiety level was such that for a time I kept a kitchen timer on my lap as I rolled around. I had it set for five minutes, and every time it went off, I'd pray, "Thy will be done." I was convinced I'd never find another attendant and I worried myself into a frenzy. Even today, whenever I begin the search, I know it's hopeless. However, the program asks me to concentrate on doing the necessary footwork and let my Higher Power take care of the rest. I advertised and manned the phone. Each evening I gazed out over the city lights and speculated about this perfect person who was going to come and serve my needs.

Arthur looked like Boris Karloff as the Frankenstein monster, except not as suave. He had been a mental patient somewhere in the Midwest. He smoked three or four packs of cigarettes a day and got through at least a case of Coke. He carried a Bible around with him so that he could quote from it on each and every occasion.

One day I noticed that Arthur had brought the groceries home in a shopping cart. "Uh, don't you think it goes a little against Christian tenets to steal a shopping cart?"

"No, John, the Lord led me to do it. The Lord told me to use it to haul the laundry down to the laundromat on Wednesdays."

Sometimes my bedroom light would snap on and there he would be, standing in the doorway in his nightshirt in the middle of the night. "Sorry to wake you, John, but the Lord has led me to read you this passage. . . ."

With the kind of nights I was having, it was comforting to hear any kind of spiritual message, even one from a lunatic at 3:00 A.M.

The walls of the apartment were actually turning yellow from his cigarettes. He had quite a collection of Jesus rock 'n' roll, which sounded like Charles Manson backed up by the Dead Kennedys, but with biblical lyrics. And if I sent him out to buy eggs for an omelet, he was just as likely to come back with oatmeal or blueberry muffins. "The Lord led me to bring you this breakfast instead."

I had gone back to college; at 2:00 A.M. one night I was up late in my chair, studying, when the phone rang. It was my landlord. Arthur, whom I had assumed to be sound asleep, had crawled out of his window, hailed a cab, and had himself driven forty miles to Damasch State Hospital, the local funny farm, where he had checked in.

Eventually the Lord led Arthur away from me.

THE HARDEST PART of the fellowship program had now begun: the action steps, designed to purge me of resentment and guilt and enable me to live my life honestly. The first chore, Step Four, was to write down a list of all the resentments I harbored, all the wrongs I had done, and all of my character defects. The first time I tried this, I had an acute anxiety attack and had to hide in bed for two days. Donny said, "Wait six months." Having just had a short glance at my personal Medusa, I was happy to oblige. I could wait half a year to be turned to stone.

In the end I was able to recall such scenes as the time I'd gotten drunk in the nursing home, picked up the phone, dialed the head nun in the middle of the night, and called her every filthy name in the book. And the times or so years before, when I'd cornered my mother in the kitchen when everybody else was out and screamed in rage, taking everything out on her, knowing just where she was vulnerable and which buttons to push.

When I got to the parts where I goaded my father, pushing and provoking until he lashed out violently at me, I was on ground where I'd always felt myself to be, genuinely, the victim. I got on the phone to Donny and said, "Goddamn it, there are certain things that I am not responsible for and that I'm not going to forgive!" But Donny always said, "There is no justification for resentment. You can't have it." Resentment leads quickly to self-pity, according to AA doctrine, and from there to booze.

Step Five required me to admit the exact nature of these wrongs to myself, to God, and to another human being. We went out to the blackberry patch again, and Donny did the listening. It took four hours, not counting time spent hyperventilating.

Step Six was the hardest of all for me. I had to become entirely ready to have my defects removed. But I didn't want to let them go and I stalled for several months. The wheelchair was an ideal pity grabber and all-purpose manipulative tool, and I clung jealously to impatience and intolerance. Since I was paying special dues, I felt I should get special privileges. And I was unwilling to let go of the anger I harbored toward my father. It had become part of my very identity.

One biblical phrase with special meaning for Donny and me in those days was "Be still, and know that I am God." I felt it had been driven into my heart and head with a sledgehammer. A quadriplegic cannot leap up and relieve his emotions by becoming frenetically active. I felt as if a huge hand had reached down out of the heavens and placed me firmly on my butt in a wheelchair while a voice said, "Just sit there and relax for fifty years. Don't get up, ever." The only chance of relief from grief, from anger, and from resentment I had was spiritual.

Slowly, slowly I began to feel some sort of presence. At last I was ready have these defects removed and (Step Seven) I asked God to do it. He is still doing it. This, like the rest of AA's Twelve Steps, is not a single event, to be gotten over with once and for all, but a process that goes on for the rest of one's life.

The Eighth Step was to draw up a list of every individual I had injured, and that turned out to be a lot of individuals. The Ninth was to apologize to them, alone, individually, face to face. I was amazed at the spiritual dynamics of this step. I'd be in the super-market, thinking about somebody I'd fucked over in high school and sure enough, there he'd be at the end of the aisle shopping for Bisquick. I'd roll up and apologize, and the person would accept the apology. Each and every time I'd feel a surge of energy.

When I started this step, I first went to my parents' house in The Dalles, on a weekend, making sure the whole family was there. I took them into my father's bedroom, one at a time, and I made amends to each of them. And to them all I made amends for the times I'd come home raging drunk and terrorized them, even forcing my father to call the police once—I could remember the terror on the faces of my little brothers and sisters, the fear in my mother's eyes, and the shock in my father's. Yet all these years I'd been justifying myself as "the black sheep of the family."

I didn't concern myself with wrongs that might have been done to me. The AA program calls it "sweeping up your side of the street." I also wasn't to concern myself with whether the people I made amends to responded or not. It was not my business to collect brownie points. A few were hostile, but many more were astonished and delighted.

I can remember going to one of the shopping malls in Portland, where, in 1968, I'd stolen a shirt. It was a beautiful shirt, the best you could buy. I went to the store's business office and asked the manager, "What can I do, can I repay you?" He said, "It'll screw up our books. Just give five dollars to charity."

That was an easy one. One of the hardest was having to go down to Mount Angel and apologize to Sister Mary, whom I'd hated all these years for kicking me out of the nursing home and sending me to Portland, where I'd rapidly sunk into late-stage alcoholism. I thanked her for her firmness and for not being one of the "enablers" who helped me continue my addiction.

Then I made a mistake and went fishing for a compliment. I said I felt I was clearing things up, spiritually, that I was finally growing, and on and on. She laughed. "Yes, you're finally growing up at age twenty-eight."

She died of leukemia two years later, undoubtedly brought on by that smart-ass remark.

Though I am sober, my basic personality has not changed.

When I finished making amends, I had a sense of enormously increased emotional strength. It was as if the whole base of my life had broadened out on the earth. And, finally, I felt the psychic din in my life quieting, the voice of my intuition growing stronger.

Housecleaning as defined by the fellowship, like housecleaning in real life, never ends. The Tenth Step demands that if I wrong somebody, I go straight out and rectify the wrong. This enforces a rigorous, habitual honesty, and that's necessary, because if a lie works, it leads to another. Soon, the liar is back to deceiving, not just others, but himself. As the pain levels increase, that person, if he is an alcoholic, will think about reaching for a bottle; in my own case, probably a fatal move.

The Eleventh and Twelfth Steps of the program ask for a lifetime of spiritual effort and service to other alcoholics. I finally understood that I must talk about my life in meetings, however it hurt. When an attractive young woman, a senior secretary at IBM, got up and admitted that she'd worked as a whore, her honesty and strength were a gift to me. These were desperate people, bent on saving their lives. So was I. And I owed them.

I learned to control my panic and, after two years, chaired meetings. I also served on the AA hotline several nights a week. The line was routed directly to my apartment, and I took calls from some very disturbed people. Sometimes I was able to find help for them and tasted the enormous satisfaction of being on the giving end for a change.

Every aspect of my life was changing. In 1979 I had a bout of the kidney infections to which quads are susceptible, that produced blood-pressure headaches, as painful as migraines. They felt like someone was sandpapering the backs of my eyes, but there was nothing the doctors at Good Samaritan, the hospital in my neighborhood, could do about them but give me painkillers. I knew that drugs, for a guy with as little sobriety as I had, could open the door to all my old behavior patterns. I decided to do without and to concentrate on the program instead. The pain became unbearable. Finally I rang for the nurse and told her to bring the needle. As she walked back to her station to get it, I made a last-ditch mental effort, reciting the Serenity Prayer with all the concentration I had. The nurse came back with the hypo on a tray, but in the five minutes she'd been gone, the pain had vanished.

No sooner had I made some gains in strength and independence than I found myself with a new attendant. Martin was a total mom. He became devoted to me to the point of driving me crazy. He loved to drive me to school, hand over my allowance for the day, pick me up on time, make sure I ate twenty-five vegetables at each meal, all while boring my friends into grease spots. His mouth never stopped.

I got a little bit of insight into his image of me one day when I overheard him on the phone. He was selling vacuum cleaners, one of about a dozen businesses he conducted out of my apartment on the side. He was using me for a hook. "Why, yes, ma'am! I can get you that model. Of course, it may take a couple of days. You see, I also take care of a poor young man who is paralyzed *from the neck down.* . . ."

Martin was not happy to see me signing up for more rehab classes, learning to cook, change my own bag, even put my pants on and off (which took forty-five minutes), and agreeing to deliver a speech at the Hilton Hotel. I relearned skills—like driving and transferring myself—that I had abandoned since Rancho. I lost a lot of weight, began to dress more carefully, and, since I felt better about myself, became a little bit of a hit again with women.

One day I was lying naked in bed. Martin must have just given me a bath because my heels were wet, giving them a little more purchase on the sheets. I had raised the bed, an electric model, into the sitting position; it occurred to me that I might be able to bring my knees up to my chest. Maybe I could assume the old sitting fetal position, the classic relaxed pose of American guys and girls around the beach bonfire or in dorm rap sessions, a posture I hadn't been able to assume for seven years.

I hung on to the overheard straps with one arm and reached down under my knees with the other to hike them closer. The wet heels kept my legs from sliding back. It worked! Eventually there I was, with my arms around my knees, very pleased with myself.

Then I noticed that something had changed in my attitude toward my body. Just at the moment it didn't seem repellent.

In fact, it occurred to me that I wasn't at all bad-looking. Sitting there with my thighs against my stomach and chest for the first time in seven years, I felt a warm flood of acceptance surge through me.

I tightened my arms around my knees and gave myself a big hug.

CHAPTER 7

For years, whenever the subject of my natural mother was raised in therapy, it was a fiasco. "Look," the psychiatrist would point out, "whenever I ask about it, you suddenly change the subject and get angry."

"Well, she was probably some little tart. . . ."

In fact I had no idea who she was. I had never known, really, who I was. All I knew for certain was that I had been abandoned. And as a result I was phobic and neurotic, very insecure, and above all, distrustful of women. A male adoptee is quoted in a recent study as saying, "I will never trust a woman until I am lowered down into my grave." So far, I'm the same. I try and try to trust women. I need tremendous attention from women, I can never get enough. Yet at a certain level I feel hostile toward them. I just know any woman I get close to is setting me up for what I fear most: abandonment.

If I were ever to have a chance at resolving such feelings, I would have to find out who my real mother was, or at least try. I had always felt that need. But all during my growing up, I was made to feel guilty about it. "You *have* parents," the argument ran. "Parents who chose you freely. That should satisfy you. That's enough." And there was the implication that my real parents, by contrast, wore the black hats because they gave me up.

My experience as a member of AA had taught me how dangerous it can be to have unfinished business in one's life. I knew it was time to face the issue of my heritage. Yet I spent some four years in recovery before I felt strong enough to confront the issue of my parentage. I knew I'd be risking everything, emotionally. I sensed I should go slowly, that I could be mentally shattered by whatever reality I might discover.

In the spring of 1981, when I was thirty years old (and still a student at Portland State University), my curiosity, coupled with a sense of being somehow incomplete, overcame my fear. My mother was exasperated: "We've told you all we know. She was a schoolteacher. She was Irish. She had red hair." My father, stoic as always, just looked saddened: "Why are you pursuing this?" So I got in touch with an adoptive-rights group and got instruction in how to conduct the search. One key suggestion was "work your caseworker down."

Oregon law forbade adoption agencies to make any but the most vague and general disclosures to adoptees. But experience had shown that with persistence, hints would be dropped, from which connections could be made. The crucial thing was to be polite but obnoxious.

That was something I felt I could do. I have always been extremely tenacious when I really wanted something, from Paula Sobaczech onward.

My agency was a branch of Catholic Charities, located on the top floor of a seedy office building in an old section of downtown Portland. My caseworker, Morton, was tall, stooped, with slicked-back gray hair and a permanent smile, as if Basil Rathbone had been cast as Uriah Heep. He sounded like Heep, too. There was little he could do; his hands were tied; he was sorry.

I visited Morton a second time a few weeks later. His hands were still tied. He said he would like to help but the most he could manage without risking his job was this statement . . . he handed over a sheet and a half of computer printout.

The printout was a general description of my parents and their background, summarized partly from details provided by my mother and partly from notes kept by nurses at the old Saint Vincent's Hospital, where I was born. It described my mother as a "pretty woman in her early thirties with bright red hair," a single person, from the Midwest. She was the youngest of eight children, and her father had died at age eighty-four of liver cancer. My father was said to be a "ruddy, good-looking man in his early thirties," a career officer in the army who "loved ballroom dancing." Two of his sisters had diabetes. Great, I thought, I could go out and order some insulin. Another noted stated that at my birth my mother was thirty-six years old, my father thirty-three. One nurse had described my mother as "refined and articulate with a keen sense of humor." Another said she was "very refined, well educated, and somewhat aloof."

Morton was beaming. Clearly he thought that this was enough to satisfy any sensible adoptee for the rest of his life. Me sensible? I was just getting used to my senses.

I began to call for appointments with Morton every week. "It's my heredity! It's my background! I'm afraid I'm going to go insane! I've got to know!" I did everything I could to ensure that he would wince at the mere mention of my name, that bending the rules a little to get rid of me would seem like an easy bargain.

On about my fourth visit toward mid-September he said, "I'll give you a hint."

"Yes! What?"

"Your mother came from a corn-growing state."

"Nebraska? Iowa?"

"I'm gonna break the law and I'll lose my job. You'll really have to go now. I'm busy." I wanted to ram a tall Iowa or Nebraska cornstalk up his ass.

It was a sadistic game, petty power at its worst. Morton would sit at his desk with my mother's file in hand. Sometimes he'd tilt it coyly toward me as if he were giving me a chance to read it over his shoulder. I strained to make out the print but never could. He was perfectly aware that I couldn't do what I wanted to do, which was vault out of my chair, break his arm off at the elbow, and read the dossier carefully while he bled to death.

Alex suggested that we just break into Morton's office and copy the file, which, he figured, was morally mine anyway. I assured him that as a last resort . . .

Instead, I went on currying favor with Morton. For some reason he was interested in my disability. I entertained him with all the gory details. All became clear when I got to my ileal conduit, the arrangement that allows me to urinate through my side into a bag.

"Really? I've got the same thing!" he said gesturing toward a bulge in his midrift, which I had heretofore chalked up to Burger King. "Only mine is a *bowel diversion*."

He was thrilled. We were nearly next-of-kin now. He wanted to compare notes about how often we emptied our bags, and so on. He was a member of a club called the Ostomaics, which I pretended never to have heard of. In fact I had. Somebody had asked me to join back at the time of my operation, but I'd had a difficult time imagining myself joining in the chitchat at the meetings:

"Boy, did my bag leak last month! What a trouble it was!"

"Really? I had a bad seal at school the other day and my shirt got soaked. . . ."

Nothing bonds like shared experience, however, and in his rush of fellow-feeling, Morton let slip my mother's date of birth.

Now my parents, dogged down by my tenacity, produced a certificate of relinquishment bearing my birth mother's signature. It was "Maggie Lynch."

My father described how Oregon law required that I be presented, formally, to my natural mother on two separate occasions, before she was allowed to sign this document. I found it nearly unbearable to imagine such a cruel scene.

I chose not to tell Morton that I had seen this document or that I knew my mother's name. My current attendant, Lou, was a Mormon and, as such, intensely interested in genealogy; Mormons expect to be one family in eternity. Lou had almost professional skills at tracing lineage, knew how to extract credit ratings, charge-card files, entries in city and country records, Social Security information. He became my ally as we conducted bogus telephone "surveys" in search of Maggie Lynch of Kansas, born July 6, 1915. At night we'd spread our notes out on the dining room table and speculate about the unknown woman we were hunting down.

I had to go slowly, to integrate each new fact into my consciousness. Even the most predictable detail—that she was Catholic or red-haired—was reality-shaking and took days to absorb. I felt silly and timid; but in fact a fantasy I'd lived with all my life was dying slowly as the real person took on shape and substance.

Lou would drive me around town to do my chores and every time we passed a boardinghouse, I'd think, Is that where my mother holed up while she was waiting to have me? Had she eaten in that restaurant, sunned herself in that park? We were convinced we had discovered what boardinghouse she had stayed in, but the register that might have given a home address—unless she used a phony—had long since disappeared.

I became increasingly preoccupied with the search. I was on an emotional roller coaster, skidding from elation to hope, frustration to discouragement. The detective part of it was fun, but always present was a subcurrent of fear. Maybe I'd never solve the puzzle. Maybe I'd never find Maggie.

At night I'd lie in bed with her specter before me in the darkness. I felt her draw closer and closer to me physically. She seemed to wear a wedding veil, through which I couldn't quite see. I awoke one night, tossing and turning, her image before me. Suddenly I felt myself being transported through the blackness. I felt myself rushing deeper and deeper, further and further, back and back until I was actually a tiny baby, just born. I felt darkness around me and I realized that I had no eyesight; but I had a sense of what was around me, such as only an infant has. There was a warm, protecting presence near me. Then, suddenly, it was gone. It vanished as abruptly as a boat disappearing over a waterfall.

I felt instead the familiar, aching, deep cold I had carried with me for thirty years. It was the icy chill of rejection, the slap on the face that meant, "You're no good." I broke down, my whole body was wracked with sobs. I cried as an infant cries, without any restraint. The infant I now was knew nothing of the social fears and conventions that might justify such an ordeal. He knew only its agony.

Later I realized that this was the moment psychoanalysts call into being with years on the couch, or therapists with exotic drugs. Somehow I had reached a catharsis, a tremendous release of grief that caused my whole body to spasm. This happened once again during the months of my search, and then I seemed to be free of it.

The hunt for Maggie Lynch had become my whole life. I talked of nothing else to my friends, the girls I dated, and, of course, Lou. Nearly every day I had him drop me off at the cathedral. I wanted to do my thinking in a place to which my real mother must have often come.

Lou and I turned up a real candidate, a Margaret Lynch of Kimball, Nebraska, who was the right age. She was Swedish, but so might I be. I took days, studying her from afar via utility-company records, credit bureaus, and so on. I compiled a dossier that would have passed FBI muster. Finally I picked up the telephone, introduced myself, and explained the circumstances of my birth. Could she be my mother?

Her laughter was kind, she was sorry to disappoint me.

I was totally deflated. I was a fool. I knew I would never find Maggie. Why was I wasting my emotional energy trying to find a woman with an ordinary name and about whom I knew almost nothing in a nation of 250 million?

I WAS STILL completing my degree in English at Portland State, a slow process since I couldn't make it to morning classes. In Chaucer, I became very aware of a sensuous brunette in the back row. I wasn't flirting with her—just checking her legs out. She never made eye contact with anybody, never looked up. But her answers to questions were articulate, even eloquent, in an old-world, very feminine way.

One day, waiting for the room to clear so that I wouldn't have to wheel my chair out in front of everybody, I made eye contact and she rewarded me with a great big smile.

A few days later, outside of class, I found some excuse to ask her a question about homework and ended by asking her out. She said she was busy but would go out with me in about ten days. A classic put-off, I thought.

But ten days later Lou said a girl named Janet had called while I was out.

We went to dinner and I fell in love. I hadn't felt anything like this in years; but I was nervous. I was sober, which meant that for the first time ever my feelings were all present and accounted for, nervousness and self-doubt included. Worse, I was in the middle of the search, in a state of increasing tension and anxiety. I avoided making love with her for almost two months, an eternity by my standards.

Even so she made me feel terrific. We made my attendants sick by constantly staring deeply into each other's eyes; when not actually together, we spent four of five hours a night on the phone with each other.

It was a glorious summer. We flew around town in my wheelchair, Janet perched on my lap in a pretty white dress. With her perfect breasts and lush tresses she got plenty of lecherous glances, much to my discomfort. I spent a fortune on restaurants: our favorite was a Greek taverna where the old proprietress would come out of the kitchen to greet us and pinch Janet's cheeks.

Sex with Janet, as I should have known, turned out to be special. We made love for hours. Janet had been raised in Africa, where her father worked for an oil company. She was relaxed about everything physical, which was a good thing. Sometimes, with no bottled confidence to keep them away, feelings of self-doubt and embarrassment washed over me and the old John Henry refused to stand up. She laughed at me and refused to let me make a big neurotic deal of it and spend days pouting and agonizing. "*We* don't have a problem, John," she'd say. "*You* have a problem."

One morning I was performing oral sex on her when the door burst open. There stood our favorite skinny homosexual, Lou, with a breakfast tray loaded with sweet rolls. When he realized what he'd burst in on, he fell to his knees in shock. Danishes flew everywhere. He scurried around on his knees scooping up buns and shouting, "I'M SORRY! I'M SORRY!" at the top of his lungs. On his way out, still on his knees, his foot caught in the door and he couldn't close it. He kept trying to pull it shut against his sneaker.

Laughter and orgasm are great bedfellows. When he had finally made his exit, Janet said, "John, you've got to promise me one thing."

"What's that?"

"That you'll have him do that *every* morning at the same time."

Everything about Janet was just right, including the way she greeted me mockingly every day with "Well, how's your self-esteem today, Callahan?" But the more perfect she seemed to me, the more old fears began to surface and familiar mechanisms click into operation. I began to see her as not so attractive after all. I told myself she didn't understand what I was doing and had become an impediment to my search for my mother. I withdrew emotionally. Finally, three months into our affair, I suggested that maybe we should both be more "open" and start seeing other people.

Janet smelled a rat. "Goddamn it, Callahan, I'm not your social worker, I'm your girlfriend! Don't try that pop psychology crap on me!" And she walked out, for good.

Once while making love I had a close call.

Fig. A. Having a good time

Fig. B. Realizing I cannot breathe

Fig. C. Jenny bears down, misinterpreting my struggle as passion

Fig. D. Panicking at the thought of suffocating

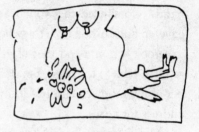

Fig. E. Release

Lou and I worked our way through a whole list of Maggie Lynches without any luck. Some fit our profile more closely than others; but one seemed a perfect fit. The date of birth was identical. She was a red-haired Catholic from Kansas. She lived alone in San Diego.

I called and went through my spiel. "Hello? I really don't know how to begin . . . I don't quite know how to put this, but there's a possibility that I'm your son."

"I never had a child," she answered wistfully. "I wish you *were* my son, though."

I had been so absolutely convinced that I didn't quite believe her, kind though she sounded. I decided to try something.

I confronted Morton with everything I had except the results of my phone call. "You've got her!" he exclaimed, throwing up his hands. Convinced the woman in San Diego was my mother, he gave up and turned over the whole file.

I took it home and that night Lou and I pored over it on the kitchen table. Here were the names and addresses of every member of my mother's family. Oddly the dossier didn't have a current address for her.

"My" Maggie Lynch had been a county auditor living near Omaha. She was the youngest of nine kids, the older ones born in Ireland, the younger ones in the United States. Her father was a farmer from County Cork. After her father's death she had stayed home and cared for her mother, and so her most marriageable years had passed her by.

She had become pregnant by an army major three years her junior. The ages of his legitimate children suggested that he was married either at the time or within a few months. At that time and place, the scandal of pregnancy would have meant ostracism and probably the loss of her job.

She had come to Portland to have me in secret. Nobody knew as much, not even her own sisters. When she left Portland, she did not return to Nebraska. She settled in Denver instead, took out a real estate license, and began an entirely new life.

I knew so much! I had eight aunts and uncles! They were Catholic! They were Irish, and so was I! I didn't have to pretend, in order to seem one of the Callahan tribe. My mother had a tremendous sense of humor, so I came by mine naturally!

I had visions of a big reunion. What a wonderful thing! They would kill the fatted calf. "We're all reconciled to it now. Come on out. Be part of the family." My whole shabby life could be left behind.

I spent several days just digesting and relishing the facts. I spent most of this time alone. I was about to meet the woman who had haunted my thoughts for years. Somehow I knew she would accept me! For months I had felt her presence growing closer and closer. Now the veil would be torn away and everything revealed.

After long discussion Lou and I settled on one of her brothers to telephone. We wanted the least chance of being stonewalled right at the outset. If the brother was at his office, his wife—an in-law—would probably answer and would be likely to be less shocked at such a revelation.

The tension was unbearable. I went into the kitchen as Lou dialed. In spite of everything my ears were straining, so I turned on both the hot and the cold water and fiddled loudly with pots and pans.

But I could still hear Lou's professionally smiling voice. "My name is Lou Ross and we're doing a survey. . . . I understand you are married to the brother of Maggie Lynch. . . ."

His cheerful patter went on for what seemed like hours. Finally he hung up, his survey-taker's smile still in place. He turned toward me.

"Your mother died in a car accident when you were twelve."

"Then why are you smiling?"

"I don't know."

I rolled out into the autumn night. It was raining, but I couldn't feel it. All my senses and emotions were deadened. I felt utterly numb and as empty as if someone had ripped my guts out. This sweet woman. . . . The idyllic relationship we were going to have. . . . It was as if I had known her all my life and she had died suddenly. I just sat there in the rain in shock wondering how I should feel. Finally Lou helped me to bed, where I turned once again to my Higher Power—this time in rage.

I'm not usually given to the little "guardian angel" fantasies common among Catholics. I don't want to make too much of the fact that at about the time she died, I started drinking, smoking, and cutting school, cheating on tests, cultivating cynicism and provoking messy fights with my father; or that I've distinctly felt an invisible hand guiding me at times, such as the moment I bottomed out on alcohol, and have thought it might be hers. But, much later, when tears finally came, I mourned her as though I had known her, on some level unexplained.

The next day I called the adoptive-rights group and told my counselor there what had happened. He said, "Quick, call your father's side." Otherwise, he warned, I was in for a prolonged depression.

Once again Lou smiled into the phone as he dialed. The number he had was in the name of my father's wife. "Hello? We're taking a survey . . ."

Lou hung up. "My God, I don't believe this!"

"What?"

"He's dead too."

My father had died of a heart attack at age thirty-six, when I was three.

I stopped going to classes and went into a virtually catatonic state for several days. I stared at the wall. When thinking at all, I thought of ending it right there with a 12-gauge shotgun. What did I have to live for? Miraculously, though, I never considered taking a drink. Instead, I slowly began to use the Twelve Steps to gain perspective and relieve the pain.

Bit by bit, sanity returned. Surely there was something I could salvage out of all this. This time I picked up the phone myself and called one of my mother's older sisters, now age seventy, living in New Mexico.

It was a mistake. When I identified myself, she told me in no uncertain terms that no such person as myself could exist: my mother had lived and died a spinster and a virgin. All the facts I had amassed had no effect on her. I tried to ignore her stubbornness and asked other questions: had my mother been artistic? Why, yes as a matter of fact . . . but then she remembered she was talking to a total stranger who had no right to ask such questions. Finally she hung up.

I tried again.

My father, whose name was John as it happened, had two legitimate children, John and Megan, who were in turn raised by a stepfather. I was delighted at the thought that I had a half brother, happier still that his son, my nephew, was also named John! I called my half brother, a lawyer, and introduced myself.

"Hi. My name is John Callahan. I'm a student at Portland State University in Portland, Oregon, and you're my half brother. We have the same father."

I marshaled all the facts. When he had heard me out, he said,

"I didn't know anything about my father. I don't remember him." He kept asking why I wanted to know these things, which obviously signified nothing in his life. His voice was cold. "You'll have to promise never to tell this to my sister. And especially not to my mother. It would kill her."

She already knew. She had received a fake "survey" call from Lou two days earlier. And she had earnestly requested that my half brother not be called. The shock would kill him, she had said.

Soon after, I received a formal letter from his law partner, a much older man who acted like a surrogate father. He listed all the damage my inquiry could do and called upon me to cease and desist. There was also a veiled threat: "Things could get very rough for you if you pursue this."

I had now announced my existence to both sides of my natural family and received identical messages: never call us again! However, I wasn't yet in a quitting mood.

Further tracking revealed, in the files of a Denver newspaper, an account of my mother's fatal accident. She had driven off a notorious mountain cliff above Denver in a car full of priests and women members of a Catholic lay order. The article mentioned that she had been a successful realtor, active in politics and (I would have expected no less) a strong Kennedy supporter. It also described her as devoted to the care of inner-city orphans.

I was able to identify the priest who had buried her and traced him to a nursing home. I was warned that he was quite senile and so he sounded. But when I said I was Maggie Lynch's bastard son, his voice suddenly became firm.

"Yes, I remember her. I buried her in '63. Your mother was an outstanding person, John. Sounds like you are, too. I'll give you the name of her best friend. It was Teresa Dugan."

Then, as suddenly as it had come, the strength and firmness

vanished from his voice, and it was to a feeble old man that I said good-bye.

Teresa Dugan had been one of the lay sisters who worked with my mother. Her initial reaction was one of anger and disbelief. "This isn't funny. Maggie Lynch never married."

"I know, but . . ."

"This is absurd. Your mother never had sexual relations with anybody. I knew your mother for many years. She never mentioned anything about you. You can't exist."

My long barrage of facts only half-convinced her. I said, "I'll send you pictures and a letter."

"Maggie Lynch was a tremendous woman, a very dear friend of mine, and I'll thank you to get off the phone and never call here again."

The next day I had my picture taken and sent it off with a complete account of what Lou and I had uncovered.

Evidently that photograph changed everything. Teresa Dugan wrote me back a letter that is still one of my most treasured possessions. "What a nice-looking boy! It's like having a piece of Maggie left on earth. . . . Your mother was the most resilient, the strongest person I've ever met." She went on and on, drawing an intimate and affectionate portrait, in effect introducing me to my own mother.

By an incredible stroke of luck, Teresa Dugan was also an enthusiastic amateur photographer. She announced, too, that she was sending me a package. When her parcel, as big as a hatbox and heavy, arrived, I gave Lou the keys to the van and told him to get lost for a while. I sat for hours with the package unopened on my lap. My God, I was thinking, this is finally the moment.

I said a prayer, took a deep breath, and ripped the package open. And there she was.

The photos showed a beautiful, red-haired woman. Her eyes shone with intelligence and humor. Here at last was the unknown toward whom, for so many years, I had directed conflicting emotions of tenderness and anger, hatred and love.

She looked a lot like me! She had my forehead! She looked like the memory of myself in the mirror. There she was, alone or (more often) surrounded by friends, holding a cigarette or a can of beer, smiling and laughing. Teresa wrote, "If she had been alive and you had found her, she would have welcomed you with open arms."

It was agony to think I'd never meet her, though adoptees who do meet their natural parents sometimes regret it, becoming disillusioned and depressed. But I knew I would have liked *this* Maggie Lynch.

Everything the photographs showed, and everything Teresa's captions said, seemed to bear upon me. She had a sense of humor. She was successful—someday I was going to be successful. The fact that she made money meant that I could make money too. She had a charismatic personality. And she was deeply spiritual in her approach to life. I was not created out of thin air. I had a heritage, and it was a fine one.

When I was a child, I sometimes screamed at my adoptive parents, "I'm going to go get my *real* mother!" Now I had done it, but not at all in a spirit of childish vindictiveness. I felt that I had gone into the search with my feelings out of control and ended it with new calmness and strength. My adoptive mother, Rosemary Callahan, had been resistant to my search, perhaps feeling threatened, but now to my surprise she said she felt the search had brought her very close to Maggie Lynch.

Like many orphans, I had been cared for during the first six months of my life by Sister Julie, a famous nursing sister in Portland, who, it was said, remembered every infant who had ever passed through her ward. My parents kept newspaper clippings about her and made sure *I* remembered *her*. Not long after Teresa Dugan's package reached me, Providence Hospital gave a fiftieth-anniversary party for this wonderful woman, and I went to pay my respects, along with hundreds of others. I was now a thirty-year-old in a wheelchair, but Sister Julie recognized me without having to be introduced.

"Why, John Callahan! I remember you! You had the bluest eyes and you were always smiling."

I told Sister Julie about my search and its conclusion, and this wise old woman told *me* what I must do next.

The cathedral was nearly empty when I wheeled myself in later that afternoon. But there was a janitor cleaning up one of the aisles, and I had him drop the coins into the box for me and light two candles. While he went to get the priest, I sat calmly in the warmth of their flames. The priest came and I arranged to have a High Mass said for both my parents. I could let them go now. That chapter of my life was closed; it was time to move on to new things.

One thing more: when anybody asks me now whether I have ever had someone close to me die, I say yes.

CHAPTER 8

In Portland many of the regular city buses are equipped with wheelchair lifts. Not long after the search for my birth parents ended, I chanced to be boarding one of these at rush hour. The bus lowers itself on its air shocks, a lift platform comes down to the curb and then rises to the level of the interior floor, slowly.

Too slowly for the patience of this particular driver, a very large, crew-cut woman clad mostly in leather. In the most abusive terms, she let me and the whole busload of passengers know just how free she was of liberal guilt about cripples who tied up traffic and put her behind schedule just as she was winding up her day and (no doubt) hankering to stomp on down to the Rubyfruit Café.

Though furious, I said nothing. Instead, that evening I drew a cartoon of a construction site protected by a big security fence. I put signs all over it: "Keep Out" "Danger" "Trespassers Will Be Prosecuted" And then, right in the middle, the biggest sign of all, "WARNING! THIS AREA PATROLLED BY LESBIANS."

I later included it in the weekly batch of cartoons I was sending to *Penthouse* magazine. After a full year of turning me down, they bought it, along with one other. Relieving frustration was one reason for drawing it, of course; I was turning everything in my life into gags, hoping to better myself. It was also true that my money had run out and my grocery budget was scarcely forty dollars a month.

I draw cartoons naturally. Rather than being learned, it just seemed to unfold, like a fifth limb. I am driven to it, and I feel it comes through from somewhere else. During the act I feel almost like an animal who is performing some primitive natural function. Someday a pathologist will be squinting through a microscope at hunks of my cadaver, and he'll exclaim, "By God, Jenkins! These are not human cells at all! These are the cells of a cartoonist!"

The first hint of all this came at age six, when I timidly showed my mother a drawing I had made of Daffy Duck, one of my lifelong role models. Nobody in the family had shown the slightest artistic talent. She was so surprised she dropped her rolling pin. After that, I got total encouragement at home. My family was thrilled about this unexpected phenomenon in its midst.

I clearly remember Sister Mary Margaret standing at the blackboard, showing the third grade how to draw a human figure: the little arches that were shoes seen straight on, the square shoulders. . . . I laughed. I could draw circles around that. A year later I would be drawing custom cartoons for Sister Mary of Joseph and illicit caricatures *of* Sister Mary of Joseph.

In fifth grade I "turned the corner" and gravitated toward the

Incorrigibles. No more model student. I joined the gang that bullied Tim Resnik, the smartest kid in school, into letting us copy his homework, not because I needed to, but to be one of the boys. At the same time, having tasted the delights of cruelty in fourth grade, I turned my hand increasingly to caricature. I made friends with another extremely funny and extroverted junior artist, Dale McCall. Together we practiced having fun at someone else's expense; naturally, we drew dirty pictures.

By high school, when not drinking, smoking or cutting classes, I worked up caricatures hard-hitting enough to strain relationships, but the payback in notoriety was worth it. There was a kid named Dotton who was from the wrong side of town. I worked up a strip, "Dotty," that lampooned his career as a "greaser." Later I pushed my friendships within the gang to the limit by such stunts as putting a tiny red penis on the tall, ectomorphic, albino Aronsen. I drew a history of the entire life of my best friend Frank Foley: His birth, the times he had to stay home from school with asthma, the moment he discovered he was lousy at sports, and so on.

An even more challenging subject was a strip describing Ralph Meyers's stroll with a rat. Stoned on acid, Ralph was walking along the street when a big rat came right out of the sewer and—no doubt noticing that this human was in a state of deep oceanic schizophrenia—decided to walk along with him. Rat and loony kid mimicked each other's subtlest expressions. We all found this hilarious.

At the time I was very much influenced by Don Martin, star of *Mad* and later of *Cracked* magazine, whose goofy, attenuated characters, their toes curled over the edge of the curb as if broken, their mouths grinning inanely, stumbled down the street toward whichever of life's disasters awaited them just around the corner. Twenty years later I still feel Martin's influence.

I also drew a lot of serious stuff. I was open to anything that would help me impress people. I walked in the woods and drew what I saw. People would say, "Look at that tree! What a wonderful broken wagon wheel!" I discovered I could sell my vignettes for good money—sixty dollars apiece. Drawing from life was a pleasure, almost a form of meditation, but it never quite satisfied me. Something was missing.

Nothing at all was missing from my nude of Mr. Wilson, my high school math teacher and a friend of my father's. I drew him in the most sexually compromising position I could imagine. I hated his guts, and after he saw the drawing, he hated mine. So did Cathy Reardon, my eleventh and twelfth-grade English teacher. I panicked as I watched my study of her boffing a goat pass from hand to hand, accompanied by a wave of laughter, through an entire all-school assembly, so that when she finally got a look at it, she knew that everyone else had too.

I received tremendous encouragement from Don Lescher, the high school art teacher, whom, I'm sorry to say, I repaid mostly with indifference. I did not want to paint, sculpt or throw pots. So he let me leave class with a drawing pad. I would walk across the campus to Aronsen's house, get stoned and listen to the Rolling Stones. Then, during the last ten minutes of the period, I would draw quick caricatures of my buddies in the house and of the people I passed on my way back to school. Mr. Lescher would say, "Ah, here's what Callahan did today," and everybody would gather around to look. It became a tradition. "Oh, yes, that's Margaret Jones, that's Mike Kelly. . . ." I got my strokes.

My *chef d'oeuvre* during this period was a two-foot-by-three-foot pencil portrait of the singer-songwriter Tom Rush, copied from an album photo. I gave it to my brother Kip for his birthday. He was moved to tears. A few years later, when I was working at the aluminum plant, I needed to impress Deborah Coker, the girl I later followed to L.A. I sneaked back home, stole the portrait from Kip's bedroom, and presented it to her as something I'd just drawn.

Much later, when I was at Mount Angel nursing home, I drew the portrait again. I couldn't apply the pressure needed for pencil anymore, so I used a ballpoint gripped in my $350 custom wrist splint. In ink it was much more impressive. I had it framed and gave it back to Kip. This time the whole family was moved to tears.

Except for a couple of caricatures at Rancho, I drew no cartoons in the years following my accident. But my portrait drawings had a cartoonlike quality. I drew student nurses, the sisters at Mount Angel, the patients. I was especially interested in Joe, my roommate, an eighty-year-old hobo who had become temporarily paralyzed when he fell off a moving train. I learned that old people are much more satisfying to draw, that each lined face has its own design. By contrast young faces are like balloons, relieved only by the little oases of eyes and mouth.

My favorite elderly subject was Marie Hulette, a society woman whose relatives had all died off and who was herself dying of cancer. She had a large private room with a view of the orchard. She hovered there in a sort of ghostly fashion, like Blanche DuBois. Once a pretty woman, with large eyes, a sculptured nose, and high cheekbones, she now looked much older than her sixty years, with dark circles under her eyes and yellow skin. The nurses told me, and Marie confirmed, that she was the niece of T. S. Eliot.

I visited her nearly every night. We both liked to watch *What's My Line?*—less a quiz show than an excuse for some witty chitchat between sophisticated New Yorkers. I loved her cynicism: "You know, John, I look at the world through jaundiced eyes." I drew her over and over as the cancer ravaged her. I watched her growing addiction to the Demerol the nurses gave her. She was always calling for another shot. I stayed with her during the final weeks of agony until, almost at the end, the priest kicked me out.

I hung one of my portraits of Marie outside the chapel. The nurses petitioned to remove it because it was so realistic, depicting her *in extremis*. Down it came.

While I was still at Mount Angel admirers arranged a show in the nearby town of Silverton—population, 3,300. I hung forty drawings. At the opening I reacted to the applause and attention by getting drunk and embarrassing everybody.

By the time I got to Portland, I was too committed to alcoholism to draw at all. I did one piece during my stay at Friendship Nursing Home: a small pen-and-ink of a beaten and dead baby, smudged. I signed it backward, mounted it on a huge mat and hung it in a show of patient art, priced at three hundred dollars.

Then I sat in the hallway and enjoyed the outrage. "What *is* this awful thing? Oh my God . . . what kind of name is Nahallac? Whoever this Polack is, he should be locked up. . . ."

After working through the steps of the fellowship and taking the big emotional risk of the search, I began to feel a huge rush of energy. Still a senior at PSU, I was sitting in class one day, with a piece of paper and a pen before me. I suddenly realized that I had been—or should have been—a cartoonist, a gag man, all along.

I doodled a cartoon to amuse the girl sitting next to me. It wasn't much of a gag: a beggar with dark glasses and a white cane and the sign "Glasses Too Dark to See Through." But I thought it was well drawn and I showed it to everybody. Then I drew another, and another. Suddenly I knew this was what I did. Within forty-eight hours I had become obsessed. I drew gags continuously and during every available waking moment. Early on, I drew a beggar-on-the-street gag that comes close to describing my own personality. The guy has about twenty tin cups spread out all over the sidewalk. His sign says, "Compulsive."

Being a cartoonist had never seemed *cool* enough to me. If I was going to be an artist at all, I wanted to be a songwriter like Bob Dylan or a novelist like James Joyce. Of course I loved to draw. I had even learned to use the old-fashioned dip pen and pot of ink, the better to emulate the little fragmentary drawings used as column fillers in *The New Yorker:* a bird feeder, a section of wrought-iron fence in a Brooklyn backyard. I became masterful at such vignettes.

But drawing by itself left me unfulfilled, even though everybody was always after me to work at it. Time after time I gave it up in favor of a more respectable ambition. I thought, I'll be a social worker, I'll be an English teacher, I'll get a law degree, something solid. But I'd actually feel nauseous at the thought of what I was giving up. (A curious fact was that if I drew nothing for a month or a year, I always found that when I went back to it, I had become mysteriously more skillful during the lay-off.)

But now, in the fall of 1981, I had confronted, and partly dealt with, the major issues in my life. At last I could give myself permission to follow my own instincts without middle-class inhibitions about status. I've noticed that successful cartoonists are rarely young. Unlike poetry or higher math, that kind of comedy seems to require a good deal of life experience. And that I had.

I came across a book by Sam Gross, the renegade star of the *National Lampoon*, with the wonderful title *I Am Blind and My Dog Is Dead*. I studied it closely. He seemed totally unafraid of the most outlandish sexual situations, disabilities, blindness. Nothing was off-limits to this outlaw. *That's* what I want to do, I thought. I never dreamed Gross would shortly become my mentor and friend.

I didn't imagine I could learn the trade from how-to books. So I tracked down the telephone numbers of Gross, Robert Mankoff of *The New Yorker*, and others and called them up. What size paper should I use? What kind of pen? How does one approach a magazine? They were taken aback, but friendly, especially when they realized that I was serious (I didn't mention that I was a quadriplegic). When I complained that I had sent a cartoon to *The New Yorker* and the editor objected that it wasn't funny, Mankoff told me, "Next time include a note explaining why it's funny." I laughed, delighted. I'd found other members of my own species. I was home.

Sam Gross is a classic gag cartoonist, revered by everybody in the field as the granddaddy of the sick cartoon. He's featured in every magazine from *The New Yorker*, to *National Lampoon*, but the latter is his home base. He is a street-smart New Yorker, and talking to him is an honor and a pleasure: "Dey wanted *all* rights ta da frog gags. I told 'em, 'Fuckyez.'"

Gross's work gave me the green light to go ahead and be crazy. He taught me that there were markets for the renegade. In fact, he became one of my first markets. I hadn't yet published in a national magazine when he called me and said, "Callahan, I'm putting together a book for Harper and Row, cat cartoons. I want to buy some from you."

I put everything on hold for a week and drew twenty, sending him my best. He bought all five, including my favorite, the cat in the Aqua-lung.

That was the first of many sales to Gross for his books; later I had the honor of appearing alongside him in *National Lampoon*.

I did a lot of imitating. If I saw a good Desert Island cartoon by someone, that would set me off, and I'd do twenty of them. I knew that I was dealing with a language, a series of conventional signs and symbols, and that languages are best learned by imitation. This language was that of the gag, the cliché situation to which the cartoonist gives a new twist. What he adds is his own vision, but it is the "common ground" of the traditional cartoon that allows him to convey that his unique personality to a public.

So I worked hard to become adept at the old stock situations: the beggar on the street, the two bums on the park bench, the bitch housewife screaming at her husband, the man dying of thirst in the desert or going mad on a desert island. I especially enjoy cartoons set on the street because the street is a common denominator, the basic turf of life where nothing is hidden and everyone passes by. There's a Sam Gross gag I particularly like. It shows a little guy walking down the street with a briefcase, one of a million robots going to work. He's walking under a street sign that says, "Curb Your Instincts." No matter how high up the economic ladder someone climbs, they can tumble down to sidewalk level and face a choice between suicide and asking strangers for

help. Enter the tin cup. I see people as, in the final analysis, help-less. Even with the confidence that comes from success, I never forget that the world remains a tough place.

I enjoy drawing that tough world and the desperation with which most people face it. Bob Dylan's song "Desolation Row," in which everyone—from Albert Einstein to the local pusher—is in the same dire straits, expresses it perfectly. That guy over there with the tin cup and the anxious face: will he score a few bucks and get his booze or bread? The whores, the society women, the bums, the executives, the hustlers and the hustled, all are up against the same wall. And their desperation is funny, exciting to me.

My Portland apartment had a huge bathroom with perfect light and I set up shop there in front of the mirror and drew continuously, trying to simplify everything, getting down to the bare-bones style I admired in Gross, in Kliban, and in a few others. Then and now, I worked on a tablet on my knees, holding the pen loosely in my right hand and bracing it with my left. I have to keep pressure on my fingers to keep them closed around the pen. My drawing comes from the shoulders, not just the arms and wrists. At Mount Angel I did a lot of competent, academic drawing just to prove to myself that I still could. That doesn't interest me today.

When I thought I had something, I'd run around the neighborhood showing what I'd done to pretty girls, bums, cops on the beat, hookers. I was Mr. Cool: "By the way, I happen to have this cartoon here. . . ." I needed the reactions. It was fun and informative, I discovered in my first two years of work, to sit in a café and watch someone pick up a local weekly in which I had a cartoon, turn to the page and react with laughter, anger or dismay. I began to understand what I could do to manipulate people's responses through a twist to the drawing here, something added to—or left out of—the caption there.

Cartooning, which I'd regarded with a certain disdain, became the center of my life. I now thought everybody should quit his job at once and become a cartoonist. I sent some gags to the Portland State University student newspaper, the *Vanguard*. They did an article about me and ran one of my gags, about a blind black beggar. I got my first hate mail. I was perceived as attacking Ray Charles and Stevie Wonder. I was a racist. Very shortly I was to be identified as a sexist, agist, fascist, communist—in fact, I'm merely cartoonist.

I had been worried about every detail of that gag. Should I draw the beggar with small round "blind man" sunglasses or with the huge white-framed ones I was seeing cool black types wear-

CALLAHAN

ing on the street? Should the guy look depressed or placid? Fat or skinny? Should there be someone else on the street, an observer, to react to him? The gag line was, "Please help me, I am black and blind but not musical." I saw I could make it even shorter. The reward was a strong reaction from the reader, which is what I aim for. I can't tolerate indifference.

The winter this book was written, *Willamette Week*, a local paper, was nearly buried under letters protesting a gag that pictures two Ku Klux Klansmen draped in their bedsheets, setting out in the moonlight to commit some atrocity. One is turning to the other to say, "Don't you just love it when they're still warm from the dryer?" A significant percentage of the *Willamette's* readership saw this as glorifying the Klan. They could not accept the suggestion that simple humans like us, concerned equally with creature comforts, wore those sheets and committed those crimes.

Then and later I was often perceived as going too far. One day I got a call from the *Vanguard*'s editor, "You better get down here. They want to kick you out of the paper." I was doing a series of amputee gags and I had sent them one about a barfly with hooks instead of hands.

I got thirty letters, and people stopped by the editorial offices to register complaints about me with the secretary: Christians, queers, teachers, foreign nationals, janitors, lab rats—all found me offensive. The student publications board convened a kind of trial. For two or three terms heated discussion involving both the faculty and the student body raged on:

To the Editor:

> I found John Callahan's cartoon in the 18 January issue of the *Vanguard* to be extremely insensitive and in the worst possible taste. . . . Comedy which aims at exposing the flaws in a person's character can be healthy. This provokes laughter which helps us to identify our faults and stimulates us to seek ways to correct them. . . . Building humor on the handicaps of a victim of some accident is, however, base and without merit. This type of laughter ridicules outcomes that were not freely chosen and conditions that cannot be reversed by the victim. Among us on this campus are a number of very brave individuals who have refused to submit to their physical limitations. . . . I applaud their courage and deplore the ugliness of spirit in John Callahan's mean cartoon.

" Sorry, mike, you just can't hold your liquor. "

The student editors rather unfairly slammed this dissenter with the revelation that I was paralyzed, which should have been irrelevant. It is to me, anyway; I reserve the right to draw gags about any group or individual, especially about self-righteous assholes who presume to defend the disabled. But if I weren't disabled, I'd find some other offensive subject matter. What is interesting is the way the writer, trying to make a simple distinction, ends up ruling out whole areas—in fact the primary areas—of comedy: combat humor, gallows humor, ghetto humor, humor based on poverty or on anything else that is not "freely chosen."

The notoriety did me no harm. I began to publish in the local papers. At the suggestion of one of my English professors I drew a version of Dante's *Inferno* as a strip. He used to have me explain my gags in class because he loved to listen to the explanations. But it felt odd to be explaining, say, an anorexia gag to a roomful of affluent, self-absorbed debutantes with glazed eyes. I felt very much like a comedian who was dying onstage. I wanted to whip out a .38 and blow the class away because their nonreaction, told me clearly: "Callahan, you missed your calling, you should have been an aluminum-siding salesman."

I began to submit gags to national magazines—*Hustler* first, because that was the most outrageous publication I could think of. At least they had the best standard reject slip. It showed a toilet with the caption, "You should draw with your other hand or become a plumber."

Also on my list of possibilities were *Penthouse* and its sister publications, *Forum* and *Omni*. I talked to people who were published there. The advice was to send ten cartoons a week, every week, always accompanied by the traditional manila self-addressed stamped envelope. When the second weekly batch bounced back to me from *Penthouse*, there was a pencil scrawl at the bottom of the printed reject slip. It said, "Holding one."

It was not exactly an acceptance; in fact, *Penthouse* is still holding that gag. They've had it so long, I've forgotten what it was. But that pencil note told me, "Keep going, you'll make it in this league." It kept me at it while spring turned into summer, and summer into fall. Batches of ten gags went out every week to *Penthouse*, *Hustler*, *National Lampoon*, and *The New Yorker*—all without acceptance.

I was accumulating enough rejection slips to build a Japanese house. But the self-doubt that had pursued me in every other aspect of my life never infected my core belief in myself as an artist. The world was just going to have to accept me, no question about it. Perhaps these editors were just temporarily confused.

One day I was at the mailbox, which of course I couldn't reach. I enlisted the aid of a small Mexican kid, a spastic who lived in the apartment complex. I noticed she was pulling out a *standard-sized* envelope from *Penthouse*. Had to be a subscription campaign, or maybe an injunction from the editor to stop wasting his time. I had tried calling editors to ask their advice, but this turned out to be a mistake. Even after he became one of my regular customers, Bill Lee of *Penthouse* answered one of my calls about a missing cartoon with "Goddamn it, I'm a busy man! I don't have a fucking minute to talk to you about this!"

As soon as I was alone in the kitchen, I began to tear at that envelope with my teeth. I dropped it; I had to call a neighbor in to pick it up for me. "Do you want me to open it for you?" "No," I said, feigning great patience. "I'll open it myself later, no big deal."

As soon as he was gone, I raced back into the kitchen and began gnawing at that envelope like an escaped convict performing his first cunnilingus in twenty years. Inside was a contract for me to sign, my first. *Penthouse* had accepted two gags. One was a very novel pirate's-hook gag. The other was "Warning: This Area Patrolled By Lesbians."

That contract meant much more to me than my college degree, which I had finally earned at the beginning of the summer. I had a purpose in life. Receiving that contract was like having an orgasm, experiencing a heroin rush, and getting a formal letter of acceptance to heaven all at the same time.

When my free sample copy of *Penthouse* arrived in the mail, it lived on my lap. I showed it to every passing stranger; I showed it to a cop, a bum, a fire hydrant. I showed it to a feminist friend and she slapped me, which I secretly enjoyed. Getting into the notorious *Hustler*, which began accepting me not much later, made my liberal acquaintances even more uncomfortable and afforded me a lot of fun. I finally stopped submitting to Larry Flynt's notorious magazine, though. His checks were always late.

Now I began to publish regularly and added *National Lampoon, Omni, Forum, Stereo Review,* the *San Francisco Chronicle,* and several others to my list. Each new contact seemed to lead to another. Even *The New Yorker* bought a gag, but they gave it to Charles Addams to redraw. There was nothing magical about all this success. A year earlier my stuff had been pretty weak. The concentrated effort required to work up more than 120 ideas in nine months had taught me a few things.

One example: I decided I was going to do a gag about a family watching television and have the caption read as a disclaimer. "The following program contains material which may be offensive to some members of your household" is the standard form. My first variation was "The following program contains language which may be offensive to members of your household who are not lumberjacks." It wasn't very funny. Next I wrote, "The following program contains language that may be offensive to some members of your fucking family." That's getting there, I thought, but not quite right.

I'm a minimalist and I like to turn a gag back on itself. So I redrew the gag with a caveman watching the set and changed the disclaimer to "Warning: The following program contains language."

I was still worrying away at this problem when, out in my wheelchair one day, I overheard two passersby react to the smell of a dumpster parked in an alley. One of them said, "Jesus, that smells bad enough to knock a buzzard off a shitwagon." I began laughing like a berserk hyena. People on the sidewalk edged away. I went around telling the gag line to everyone I knew. Back home I painstakingly drew and redrew the cartoon until it was a perfect fit with the final gagline.

That's the typical evolution of one of my gags. And, as often happens, there was a by-product: the caveman gag.

Spanking is out of fashion in liberal circles these days, which is a shame, because many kids are growing up without ever hearing that best of all bullshit clichés, "This is going to hurt me a lot more than it hurts you." I drew many versions of that one before I settled on a rather elaborate, Rube Goldberg solution.

"This is going to hurt me more than it hurts you!"

That approach hadn't worked, though, with a gag I had just finished for *Forum*. The situation was a patient in a doctor's office and the cliché was "It hurts when I go like this." I began with a machine like those Wile E. Coyote of *Roadrunner* fame builds to punish himself when he's been stupid. A boot mounted on a stick kicks the patient when he pulls the string. But it seemed flat. I redrew the gag with the patient shooting a big pistol at himself, with the bullet flying through a cartoon door in his head. It was too cute, not gritty enough.

The next attempt showed the patient flinging himself off the examination table, about to smash himself on the floor. That was better, but the gagline just didn't call for something so oddball or neurotic. What finally worked was something more connected to ordinary human experience.

"It huvts when I go like this!"

The whole art of the gag is to give a "different" twist to the expected, the normal. Several people have told me, "Callahan, I laugh at your cartoons and at the same time I feel guilty for laughing." The other day a guy introduced himself to me. He was a psychiatrist at the University of Oregon Health Sciences Center. He said, "I love your work," and then added, "I'm a sick fuck too."

Some cartoonists wake up in the morning and say, "What a beautiful day—I think I'll draw a desert-island gag." I'm more likely to wake up in the morning and say, "What a beautiful day—I think I'll draw an armless proctologist who has his patient bent over the examination table. I'll have the doctor say, 'I'm sure you'll find my technique for rectal examination somewhat different in that I am gay and have no arms.'" So it seems natural to me that people hold up crucifixes to ward me off when I come down the street.

I'm gifted with a natural "gag sense," which allows me to invent twists that somehow reflect back on the original cliché. I love the old gag about the man in the electric chair. The warden hands him a roast and says, "Would you mind holding this? My wife's oven is on the blink." Of course I immediately felt compelled to top it.

" First chance I've had to sit down all day !! "

I agree with Sam Gross's opinion that the purest cartoon is the sight gag. Sometimes sight gags get pretty complicated. In one of mine Jesus Christ is walking on the waters of Galilee, his eyes turned heavenward, a beatific expression on his face. But behind him in the boat Peter and the rest of the disciples are gesticulating frantically. For they can see what he can't: floating in the water just in front of him is a banana peel.

But a gag is always better if it's simple enough to be "read" in one glance, like my Martian gag.

CALLAHAN

I'm as much a writer as an artist, though, and for me generally the gag line comes first. In my apartment the TV is on all the time, like a respirator. One day an old Errol Flynn movie was on as I worked, and a line of dialogue floated into my consciousness: "Don't be a fool, Billy!" I thought, Boy, there's a fine old cliché.

I try to keep the reader's attention focused on the idea, not the image or the language. If a gag seems particularly strong, I draw it in a deliberately offhand, crude fashion to underline that strength. The contrast can be powerful. I have a friend who is very beautiful. But her beauty is given an exceptional power by the fact that she is in a wheelchair. Bob Dylan chose to sing the very powerful lyrics of "Don't Think Twice" or "Blowin' in the Wind" in a tired, scratchy voice backed by rudimentary guitar. I can draw beautifully if that's what's called for. But it almost never is. A clown's job is to be grotesque, so he wears baggy pants and outsize shoes.

" Don't be a fool, Billy ! "

In fact for a while I had a radio program in which I presented cartoons without any drawings at all. I'd say, "This is John Callahan with the cartoon of the day. There's a cliff, and a blind man is being dragged over it by a little furry animal on a leash. And as he

sails into space, he thinks, Why did I buy a seeing-eye lemming?"
A good gag should be freestanding.

But with drawing I can add another dimension, I can convey
the nobility of the human animal caught in an oppressive world.
My characters look round-shouldered, beaten, abused. There is
shock and disillusionment in their eyes. They could be Kurtz, in
Conrad's *Heart of Darkness*, whispering, "The horror. The horror."
In my Crucifixion, Jesus underlines that aspect of humanity.

Suicide is a powerful subject for comedy. But it is even more
powerful if it is shown against a backdrop of ongoing, uncaring
life. One of my "jumper" cartoons shows the act over, the poor
guy splattered all over the sidewalk. An efficiency expert is passing with a clipboard and stopwatch.

Comedy is the main weapon we have against "The Horror."

With it we can strike a blow at death itself. Or, at least, poke a hole in the pretentious notion that there is something dignified about it.

Recently I have begun to do longer pieces—posters and two-to-four-page spreads that allow me to develop themes and characters. With the support of a local paper, *The Clinton Street Quarterly*, I have told the story of my disability in "The Lighter Side of Being Paralyzed for Life," my alcoholism in "Callahan Unbottled," and my sex life in "My Sexual Scrapbook," as well as long treatments of adolescence and Catholicism. Doing these spreads is like producing and directing a small film. In fact one of them, "A Nuclear Christmas," is now being considered for an animated short by a film company in England. They must have strong stomachs. In this parody of "A Visit from Saint Nicholas" Santa is a mutant. He keeps losing limbs and growing new ones. "I've seventeen ears, and more that keep growing. The amount I'll end up with, there's no way of knowing."

"If you'd jumped off the seventh story instead of the twelfth you'd have achieved the same effect and saved 3.01 seconds."

The first of these features was drawn in response to *Clinton Street Quarterly* editor David Milholland's request that I "Do something personal." The idea to do something about my injury and the title came to me instantly. I more or less wrote the piece on a napkin in the café where we were talking.

For it I developed a persona, a little guy with a guilty expression and hair that stands up in three unruly prongs that (unconsciously, I swear!) are not unlike Woody Woodpecker's crest. He is dwarfed by everyone around him. Even his girlfriends are huge. Partly he's me as I was as a kid, showing off even at age six as the stand-up comedian of the family and scandalizing them with an unvarnished takeoff of my grandfather's alcoholic mannerisms. Partly, too, it's me seeing the world at areola level from my wheelchair. In any event, I'm tall, and I don't look guilty. I just finished a drawing of two paraplegics parked together on the sidewalk watching a tall man walk by. One says to the other, "You'll never get *me* up there!" Partly the little guy, who turns up in most of these features, is all of us, dwarfed by all our problems and cowed by an endless supply of blowhards and bullies who want to tell us what to do.

"Lighter Side" won some awards and attracted hundreds of letters and phone calls. I sent it to *Penthouse,* which by then had been publishing me for two years. They called me up. "We'd like to talk to Mr. Callahan. . . . You've got to be kidding! This is actually autobiographical? You *are* paralyzed?" I had never mentioned it to my clients. They bought the spread instantly, but three years later it is still being "held."

I am sometimes labeled as part of a Northwest school or movement in cartooning, comprising Lynda Barry, Gary Larsen, Matt Groening, Jim Blashfield, and Bill Plympton, among others. Sometimes the list is extended to include writers, notably Todd

Grimson and Katherine Dunn, whose wit is also more than a little macabre. Something about these gray, misty mornings, maybe, infuses our work with a grim but hilarious tone. It has also been suggested that living here, far from the trendoids of New York or L.A., we are like a bunch of exiles, looking in at America from the outside.

I don't know about all that. I view my career as having passed through three periods. First came my "black" period. Then as I developed, I entered a "black" period. Now my horizons have widened, and I feel myself to have passed through to a third or "black" period. God knows what comes next.

TODAY MY MIND resembles a Venus's-flytrap, always poised and ready. If a gag even comes close, I snap shut on it, and I exclude nothing. At the moment I am obsessed with the millions on our planet who are literally starving. I won't leave this alone. I bedevil the food neuroses of the affluent: "The Anorexic Café—Now Closed 24 Hours A Day." Or the two bulimic girls walking along the sidewalk: "No wonder you feel bad! You haven't thrown up anything all day." Even harder-hitting is the gag about the day they delivered planeloads of Chinese food to Ethiopia, and everybody was hungry again an hour later. Now that's a concept worthy of Sam Gross! I'm working on it. Frankly I don't care if gags like that get me run out of town by a mob with pitchforks and torches, or if they pin a medal on me.

Not that I am insensitive to criticism, far from it. I've been worried for days about a letter to the editor that was just printed in a Tallahassee, Florida, paper that carries my work. The writer identified himself as director of community relations for a local hospital.

Editor:

Regarding the drawing by "Callahan" in which the leader of a posse somewhere in the desert comes upon an empty wheelchair and says to his cohorts, "Don't worry, he won't get far on foot" . . .

I'll call it a drawing instead of a cartoon because "cartoon" implies or promises comedy or satire. And I'll call it insensitive and thoughtless, since instead of any humor, the drawing in a few scrawled strokes tries to undermine all the remarkable good that's been accomplished in the past several years toward better understanding of, respect for, facilities for, and opportunities for the handicapped and physically disabled.

"Callahan" owes several million people in this country an apology. . . .

Sorry, folks.

CHAPTER 9

I n the early 1980s, toward the age of twenty-nine, I was beginning to see the possibility of making a sober, middle-class living
in the profession of my choice. Solvency and self-respect were
just around the corner . . . or would have been except for one tiny
catch: I was not allowed to keep any of the money I made. Not a
dime.

Not long after my accident, while I was still in rehabilitation
at Rancho Hospital, I received an insurance settlement of about
$100,000. Half of that went as a reimbursement to MediCal; the
other half, paid in installments, supplemented the tiny Social Security Disability Insurance (SSDI) benefits to which I was en-
titled, as an ex-worker. So I was able to stay off Welfare for five
years.

Even drunk, I husbanded that money as long as I could. Maybe I sensed what was coming. The day I joined the ranks of Welfare clients was, ominously, also the day my used van finally gave up the ghost. Now I'd never be able to afford another.

Growing up in The Dalles, true redneck country, I couldn't help but assimilate the prevailing negative attitude toward Welfare. The word *bums* was always appended. I had just begun to enjoy the psychological freedom that came from settling some major life issues: alcohol addiction, parentage, career. Now I was to enter another form of total dependence. Not only that, but I quickly discovered that the Welfare system tends to make everyone concerned feel like a victim. Not only the clients, but also the caseworkers and administrators feel they are being "had." No matter how well meaning they may be at the start, all concerned tend to become hostile and embittered. I was no exception.

My SSDI entitlement was just over $600 a month. According to Welfare, that was too princely a sum. They required me to hand over $200 a month as a partial reimbursement for the $800 I was allotted for daily and weekend attendants. My rent, for a small one-bedroom, ground-floor apartment, consumed a further $325. The $75 that remained was real whoopee money. All I had to make it cover were electricity, phone, groceries, clothing, drawing supplies, envelopes, postage, copying, haircuts, dental bills other than emergency ones, and food for my cat.

Every month Alex or Lou and I would sit at the kitchen table and try to decide what combination of rice, beans, ramen noodles, potatoes and day-old bread would last the longest with the least damage to my system. I can remember, one month when we miscalculated, having to live for several days on outdated liverwurst spread, eaten straight out of the plastic wrapper.

Much worse, though, was having to get a voucher from Welfare to collect a charity parcel from Loaves and Fishes or Saint Vincent de Paul, a few canned goods, a block of cheese, or a bag of stale baked goods. There I'd be, along with the rest of the permanently indigent, lined up in the rain for a handout. I only let this happen four times in ten years. Mild starvation was preferable to such utter humiliation.

So I was very motivated to make it big in the world of cartooning. During my first two years in the national market, I made five thousand dollars. When those first checks started to arrive, I was ecstatic. I took off downtown and bought the first decent-looking clothes I'd worn in a decade. I paid bills, bought some food for the house, got a haircut. I got things cleaned up and taken care of for a while.

But with modest success came modest fame. Stories about me appeared in both local papers and on all three network television affiliates. Welfare noticed. Shortly I received a letter informing me that I would lose all my benefits unless I paid that money over to Welfare. They didn't say *when*; they just hung the threat over me like the Sword of Damocles. Somehow, I wasn't as enthusiastic during the third year of my national career.

Uncertain as any artist's life is, I'm pretty confident that I can make my own living if I am given the chance. Not just food, clothing, and shelter, but even the special expenses of a quadriplegic could be paid out of my own pocket. What a victory that would be! My wheelchair, a $5,000 item, is pretty well used up in two years. That's over $200 a month. Repairs and maintenance add another $75 or so. Then there's the electric bed, also $5,000 but with a lifespan of four years, $100-plus a month. Urological supplies and medications, $200 to $300 more. And $800 for attendants. That's an unavoidable $1,475 a month for bills that are just not there for able-bodied people. Yet I know I am capable of it.

But even then, I'd be licked, because I would have lost Medicaid. No private health insurer I'm aware of will sell a policy to a quadriplegic, and no wonder. I am certain to need hospitalization from time to time. My body has to be tricked into continuing as it is through a regime of continuous therapy. Not all systems are "go": I can't regulate my internal temperature. On a really hot day I have to dart from shadow to shadow and from water fountain to water fountain, like a lizard, or I'd perish of heatstroke. I'll always have liver and kidney problems. I am far more prey to skin conditions and infections than is the ordinary person. So, deprival of health insurance would, in effect, be my death warrant.

The United States, almost alone among the developed nations, has no public entitlement for health care. Instead, we have special programs for the elderly (Medicare) and the poor (Medicaid). Anybody with a major disability had better be one or the other. The system, it seems, wants me to stay poor, at least until I get old.

The trouble is, I'm not very good at being a poor person. I lack some of the necessary skills and abilities. For example, once I moved into Section 8 government housing, so I could get a rent subsidy. I had been getting a $40 "exception" for my rent, which meant I could keep that much more of my SSDI payment each month, because I needed a ground-floor apartment within a certain distance of grocery and drug stores. Now my total rent fell to only $112 a month, a big advantage.

I noticed that quite a few of my fellow tenants in the government housing were wearing ski masks. That made me apprehensive. Sure enough, as soon as word got around that the new tenant was a cripple, neighbors started dropping by for a chat—and to shop for anything that might be lying around loose. They stole my stereo, my TV, my VCR, and undoubtedly would have taken my wheelchair had they known how to fence it. An able-bodied poor person would have been able to reciprocate, perhaps by carving the neighbors up with a straight razor. I lacked the necessary dexterity.

To save body and soul, I moved back into a private apartment. Welfare promptly notified me that, since I'd left subsidized housing voluntarily, I was no longer eligible for the $40 rent exception.

A Welfare client is supposed to cheat. Everybody expects it. Faced with sharing a dinner of Tender Vittles with the cat, many quadriplegics I know bleed the system for a few extra dollars. They tell their attendants that they are getting $200 less than the real entitlement and they pocket the difference. They tell the caseworker that they are paying $100 more for rent. Or they say they are broke and get a voucher for government cheese.

I am a recovering alcoholic. I have opted to live a life of rigorous honesty. So, I go out and drum up business and draw as many cartoons as I can; I even tell Welfare how much I make! Oh, I'm tempted to get paid under the table. But even if I yielded to temptation, outfits like *Penthouse* and *Omni* are not going to get involved in some sticky situation. They keep my records according to my Social Security number, and that information goes right into the IRS computer. Very high profile and unpauperlike.

Lastly, as a Welfare client I'm expected to genuflect before the caseworker. Deep down, caseworkers know that they are being shined on and made fools of by many of their clients, and they expect to be kowtowed to in compensation.

I'm not being contemptuous. Most caseworkers begin as college-educated liberals with high ideals. But after a few years in a system that practically mandates dishonesty, they become like the one I shall call Suzanne, a slightly overweight cop in Birkenstocks. Not long after Christmas last year Suzanne came to my apartment on one of her bimonthly inspections and saw some new posters hanging on the wall. "Where'd you get the money for those?" she wanted to know.

"Friends and family."

"Well, you better write it down, by God. You better report it. You have to report any donations or gifts."

This was my cue to grovel. Instead, I talked back. "I bummed a cigarette from someone down in Old Town the other day. Do I have to report that?"

"Well I'm *sorry*, but I don't make the rules, Mr. Callahan."

Suzanne tries to guilt-trip me about repairs to my wheelchair, which is always breaking down because Welfare won't spend the money to maintain it properly. "You know, Mr. Callahan, I've heard that you put a lot more miles on that wheelchair than the average quadriplegic."

Of course I do. I'm an active worker, not a nursing-home vegetable. I live near downtown so that I can get around in a wheelchair. I wonder what Suzanne would think if her legs suddenly gave out and she had to crawl to work.

Spending cuts during the Reagan administration dealt malnutrition and misery to a lot of people, not just me. But people with spinal cord injuries felt the cuts in a unique way: the government stopped taking care of our chairs. My last chair never fit. I was forced to sit in a twisted position that led to a series of medical complications. But Welfare refused to replace it.

Each time it broke down and I called Suzanne, I had to endure a little lecture. "Didn't that break down last week? Are you sure you're not being a little hard on that chair? I just don't know if we can go about fixing it. Our budget has been cut, too, my friend."

I learned to curb my natural sarcasm on such occasions. It got me nowhere. Suzanne had undoubtedly been told to hold repairs down to some arbitrary quota. Being nasty over the phone had become part of her job.

Finally she'd say, "Well, if I can find time today, I'll call the medical worker."

Suzanne then started the red tape flowing. She was supposed to notify the medical worker, who made an assessment. Then the medical worker called the wheelchair-repair companies to get the cheapest bid. Next the medical worker alerted the main Welfare office at the state capital in Salem. They pondered the matter for days. Finally, with luck, they called back and approved the repair.

During the Carter administration I would call in, and somebody would stop by within an hour or two and fix the chair. Under Reagan I'm flat on my back. I'd give anything for a service arrangement or a spare chair so I wouldn't have to go to bed for days.

I have even more fun if the breakage happens when I'm out. Flying down the street, I'll hear the telltale clunk. The chair will roll out of control and smash up against a building or just quietly grind to a halt, completely dead. I sit there roasting, or freezing, or getting soaked depending on the season, blowing an appointment with an editor or a friend. Eventually somebody consents to give me a push. Then, if they put my quarter in the payphone, I'm able to call one of the wheelchair repairmen and say, "Look, I'm downtown and my chair is broken, can you do something?"

"Well, we can't do anything until we get an okay from your caseworker. So try to get hold of her and call me back."

So I accost another stranger, who dials the Portland Welfare office for me.

"Oh, Suzanne left at two o'clock today."

"Can I talk to her supervisor?"

"He's not in the office today."

"I've got an emergency here," I say, trying to describe my situation. But I am cut off with, "Well, you'll just have to call back tomorrow, we're not able to help you at this time."

So I call back the wheelchair company.

"Sorry, but they've really cracked down on us. We can't make a move until the funding is in order."

Finally I call Broadway Cab. Half an hour later the lift van arrives and takes me the twelve blocks home. The cabbie pushes me up the sidewalk and into my apartment. He positions me near the urine bucket and puts the phone in my lap. I try to mend fences with the editor I've stood up. I try to reach my attendant, who is gone for the day, and the neighbors, who are not home. I sit there until the night attendant shows up at 10:00 P.M. unable to turn on the TV, get a drink of water or move one inch for six hours. Sometimes I get a joke out of it.

Ultimately Welfare must have spent ten thousand dollars fixing that lemon of a chair. It would have been cheaper for them to buy me a new car.

When Welfare learned I was making money, Suzanne's visits came every other week instead of every other month. She poked into every corner of the apartment in search of contraband Cuisinarts, unregistered girlfriends, or illegal aliens serving as butlers and maids. She never found anything, but there was always a thick pile of forms and affidavits to fill out at the end of each visit.

"Mr. Callahan, you've simply got to understand the gravity of the situation. Your cartoon earnings could cause your benefits to be terminated!"

"How do I avoid that?"

"I'm not sure . . . but it doesn't look good for you."

"Well, then, who do I speak to about the specific regulations on this?"

Suzanne didn't know. One day I simply called her superior and asked if he could tell me where to start. "Well, Mr. Callahan, we have reason to believe that you are a bit of a shady character. I'm fairly certain your benefits will be terminated."

There is no provision in the law for a *gradual* shift away from Welfare to self-support. I am a free-lance artist who is slowly building up his market. It's impossible to jump off Welfare and suddenly be making two thousand dollars a month, even if I could solve the health insurance problem. But I would love to be able to pay for some of my services and not have to go through a humiliating rigamarole every time I need a spare part.

Over the years I have learned that Welfare is never, ever wrong. Whatever happens, it is always the client's fault. It seems that no one at the agency is ever fired for failure to perform. But if I am even a day late sending in the two hundred dollars I must pay them to be eligible for an attendant, I hear about it, pronto. "We will terminate your benefits if that check isn't here immediately, Mr. Callahan."

Every letter or form from the agency seems to begin the same way, with minor variations:

"Your benefits are being terminated unless . . ."

"Your benefits *will* be terminated if . . ."

"Funeral arrangements following your suicide are being made at Murphy Brothers Chapel and your benefits will be terminated unless . . ."

When a caseworker crawls into the sack with her husband, she probably murmurs, "Your benefits will be terminated unless I have an orgasm this time, hon."

On the other hand, Welfare is perfectly happy sending my monthly Medicaid card on the last day of the month for which it is valid. They don't mind at all if I have to use my own money in the meantime, for medication or urological supplies, or a doctor's appointment.

Welfare workers never return your phone calls. They are always out in the "field." Somewhere there must be a huge pasture with five thousand caseworkers down on their hands and knees, grazing. Ask a question, and you get no answer. Ask to speak to the supervisor, and you'll get a runaround. If you persist and actually get to speak to the supervisor, *he'll* give you the runaround. One of my former caseworkers—not Suzanne—is now a buddy. He revealed that any assertive client was written up in his file as an unstable troublemaker.

Welfare workers have always told me I worry too much. Back before the Reagan administration cut me off Food Stamps, I used to worry about getting cut off Food Stamps. Suzanne told me not to worry. "Besides, you're only eligible for ten dollars' worth of stamps. Do you really want to bother filling out all these forms?"

Ten dollars may be nothing to *you*, dear lady, I thought. They kept shrinking Food Stamp eligibility, though. I think the final rule was something like, "Only those quadriplegics who can roll their tongues and who have one or more female siblings living within five hundred feet of a nuclear reactor will be eligible for Food Stamps." In any event, I wasn't even close to eligible.

I do worry about the rules. In Welfare, the rules change constantly. One month I am allowed to make seventy-five dollars, the next month, nothing. I must order my medical supplies once a month. Then, once every two months. Soon again, back to once a month. Recently I learned that my weekday attendant was no longer allowed to work the weekend position. At least one day a week the work must be done by someone else. Nobody wants to learn a complicated and stressful task like that for one day's pay.

One rule dictates that my spouse, if I had one, could not work as my attendant. As a result many quadriplegics do not marry. This can present a problem, however, for people like my friends Nick Kellog, a quad, and his wife, Nancy, who are devoutly religious and would not live together in sin.

Like any bureaucracy with complicated rules, Welfare constantly creates and eliminates "exceptions" to those rules. Quads often have strained kidneys and need extra protein. So an exception allowed me to keep a little more money to supplement my diet. Then came a note that the exception had been cut off retroactively. I owed Welfare for meat and cheese I'd bought with my own money and already eaten. I volunteered to come over to the office and throw up, but they wanted cash.

Another month they canceled an exception for dental care "except for emergencies." To save money, they eliminated prevention. By the time my teeth are rotten enough to become eligible, the tab will be enormous. Not long after, they eliminated the exception for any eyeglasses other than the cheap ones that make you look like Admiral Tojo. Cheap frames, of course, break frequently.

When we quads and paras trade Welfare experiences, it becomes clear that we're all being told different stories. The rules seem to be whatever the Suzannes and their administrators want them to be. There is only one constant: break them and you can get terminated. So I ask questions.

"Suzanne, how can I be penalized by making X amount this month?"

"John, you worry too much about your benefits."

"But what's the rule on this?"

"Oh, there's no rule, it's just common sense. You worry too much."

I always feel like asking, "If we were dealing with *your* basic needs—your phone, your garbage, your laundry, your rent, your food, your attendants—would you be nervous about losing the whole thing with one false move?"

Instead, I go around with a sickening lump of nausea in my gut. Am I going to end up in a federal or state nursing home, reeking of urine? Am I going to end up on the street like the Bakkers? You bet I want to know what the rules are. Absurd as it may seem, my success as a cartoonist makes me feel like a renegade, a culprit. When a check comes in from a magazine, I look at it and part of me says, "Way to go, Callahan! You're getting published!" Actually it was a rather special honor when I got into *Penthouse*. They pick up one new cartoonist per year, worldwide. But the other half of me says, "Watch out, motherfucker! You're cheating the system. You're cheating Welfare. You shouldn't have this money. Better put it in an envelope and run it right down to Suzanne."

Behind every sale lie dozens of false starts, a phone bill that runs $150 to $300 a month, postage, photocopying, art supplies, energy, sweat, loss of sleep, bowel stoppage. I'm supposed to fork my check over and say, "Sorry about that. I shouldn't have made this money. Here it is back."

One day Suzanne pinched my spare tire and said, "Well, it sure looks like your attendant's feeding you pretty well. You don't look like you're starving to death." My diet is mainly cheap carbohydrates because that's all I can afford; additionally it is very hard for a quadriplegic, especially in his thirties or older, to find ways to burn calories and stay trim.

Such insensitivity is typical. As usual I knuckled under and bore this sneer in silence, reminding myself that caseworkers like Suzanne get that way because of the insane administrative structure they work under.

I know I am lucky to live in a country where I wasn't thrown out to the wolves when I broke my back. I don't have to beg with a tin cup, because I did get some help from the government. I want to distinguish sharply the professional and courteous treatment I have always received from Social Security from the inadequately funded and state-administered Welfare program. The plain fact is, though, that until quite recently, when I began to be perceived as something of a minor media threat, Welfare treated me like a bum.

So I have had to make conscious efforts to build up my self-esteem, to tell myself that I am a good person, that I am trying, that I am as good as the average guy working down at the 7-Eleven or over at IBM. I have to tell myself that because the daily message from Welfare has been that I am one more degenerate whose family has lived on the dole for generations.

A year or so ago I began hearing about something called a "Plan of Support," an obscure regulation written entirely in legal gibberish, no doubt to keep most clients from trying to take advantage of it. A "Plan of Support" allows certain Welfare recipients to earn and keep some income if certain criteria are met. For example, I might be able to keep enough for a part-time secretary or some travel expenses.

In effect this plan would give me permission to pay for the overhead expenses of my business with money I earned. To me, this would be a godsend. There are many tasks I can't perform because my fingers are mostly paralyzed. For example, it's extremely difficult for me to send new material to my major clients. They are running cartoons already "held" from previous mailings. I need someone to come in and duplicate most of a year's output, with copies going to my agent, my clients, a fireproof master file, and a working file. I need a log kept of who has what. I need billings and receipts straightened out. I need to order tax records.

In the past, girlfriends have sporadically tackled this job, until, understandably, they got tired of it. My attendants are too stressed by what they already do. I need a secretary.

I can't write, or edit what I write, on a typewriter. I need a personal computer with a keyboard suited for what my hands can do.

And, like anybody who sells, I occasionally need to meet face-to-face with my customers. I can't compete in the world's toughest marketplace, the New York publishing world, as a disembodied voice on the phone. Not forever, anyway. Yet right now that's how I'm dealing with *Penthouse, Omni, National Lampoon, Forum, American Health, Vanity Fair, The New Yorker* and a baker's dozen of newspapers.

My agent and I sat down and wrote an application for a "Plan of Support" according to the complicated regulations, which we had translated for us by a volunteer lawyer. So far as I could discover, no one in Portland had ever done this before.

I gave the finished plan to my caseworker. She passed it to her supervisor. He passed it to somebody at the head office, who passed it to somebody else, who probably passed it through his colon into a toilet, which passed it into a river, which passed it into a sea. *It flat fucking disappeared!* Nobody has any idea what happened to it. The volunteer lawyer is still trying to find it, nine months later.

I want to get ahead. I have the talent, the ability, the desire, and the moxie to do it. I have twice the drive of the average able-bodied person. What I am being told by the Welfare system is, no, we won't let you do it.

I don't have time to march around town with a placard that says, "Unfair to SSDI Quads." I already sacrifice a good part of my day to my morning program. Much of the rest of the time I'm sick or immobilized by one thing or another. I've tried everything I can think of. There is no effective lobby for quadriplegics, but I've given what time I could to the National Spinal Cord Injury Foundation. I've written or called all my state and federal congressmen and senators. I've attempted to get some legal pressure brought on the system, but "poverty law" is unattractive to most lawyers because it isn't remunerative. The very distinguished attorney who is working with me now is a rare bird indeed.

There needs to be some ombudsman or legal resource for all Welfare clients, because the system so easily lends itself to abuse by the givers as well as by the recipients. Welfare sent Suzanne to snoop around in my apartment the other day because I was using a larger than usual amount of urological supplies. I was indeed: The hole that was surgically cut in the wall of my abdomen has changed size, and the connection to my urine bag had been leaking.

The implication of her visit was that I was cheating. What did they think I was doing, selling urine bags to Greeks as wineskins?

While she was taking notes, my phone rang, and Suzanne answered it. The caller was a state senator, which rattled Suzanne's cage a little. Would I sit on the governor's advisory board and try to do something about the thousands of Welfare clients who, like me, could earn part or all of their own living if they were allowed to do so, one step at a time?

Hell, yes I would! I'd sit on a goddamn emery board if I could help change some of these medieval rules that have given me gray hair and a heart murmur! Someday handicapped men and women will be thriving under a new system based on incentive and encouragement. They will be free to develop their talents without guilt or fear—or just hold a good steady job.

I hope to see it happen before my benefits are finally terminated by the Great Caseworker in the Sky.

CHAPTER 10

"People like you are a real inspiration to me!"

How many times has this happened to you: You're in a public toilet with a quadriplegic. Suddenly he turns to you and says, "Say, my hands are a little numb. Would you mind catheterizing me?"

If you feel at a loss in this situation, you're not alone. In the years since my accident I've had plenty of opportunity to study the way able-bodied people behave around the maimed. Few display any *savoir faire*.

Often I've found myself in a slow elevator with a crowd of people who first stare at me and then look away. I try to break the ice with a pleasant remark, such as, "Damn! I *knew* I should have crawled up the stairs!" Suddenly everyone seems to take a vivid interest in fake oak panelling.

Experiences like these have led me to create my award-winning guide, *How to Relate to Handicapped People.* Take a few minutes to study it now. And remember, there's a quiz at the end.

I.   In the past, handicapped people weren't an issue because they weren't seen around much. They were "shut-ins."

II. Today, handicapped people are more visible than ever. Yet people are often still uncomfortable around them. In an attempt to be appropriate, people tend to overcompensate.

III. The first thing to realize is that the handicapped are just like you or me!

(SOME ARE HAPPY)   (SOME ARE DEPRESSED)

(SOME ARE COOL)   (SOME ARE FAT)

(SOME ARE GEEKS)

IV. The correct way to approach a handicapped person.

V. Don't be afraid to ask questions—children are spontaneous
and uninhibited in their curiosity. Take a lesson from them. . . .

VI. When should you help a handicapped person? (Many people have expressed anxiety regarding this issue.) Basically you must use your own judgment.

BE PREPARED FOR THE OCCASIONAL PERSON WHO WILL RESENT YOUR ATTEMPTS AT HELP:

SOMETIMES IT WILL BE QUITE OBVIOUS THAT A HANDICAPPED PERSON NEEDS YOUR HELP— NOT YOUR POINT OF VIEW!

OTHER TIMES YOU MAY WISH TO ASK THE PERSON IF HE NEEDS ASSISTANCE...

VII. Handicapped people can be helpful to you sometimes. Let them! Handicapped folks get a special sense of usefulness when they are on the helping end of a situation.

ON THE SUBWAY

VIII.   If you enjoy a handicapped person's company, what's next?

IX. Over the years many myths have arisen. Here are a few we've
    heard one too many times!

X. Odds 'n' Ends—How to communicate with someone who has a speech problem.

RELAX, LISTEN CAREFULLY FOR A FEW MINUTES...

IF YOU DO NOT YET UNDERSTAND...

TRY AGAIN TO LISTEN; RELAX, AND CONCENTRATE:

SOMETIMES THIS GETS VERY DIFFICULT...

IF, AT THIS POINT, YOU'VE SIMPLY MADE NO HEADWAY, HAND THE PERSON A PEN AND PAPER:

YOU WILL FEEL A DEEP SENSE OF GRATIFICATION IN HAVING FINALLY COMMUNICATED...

NOW THAT YOU'VE brought yourself up to date, let's review what you've learned. (For correct answers to these questions, send a check for $25 payable to *CASH* to the address below.)

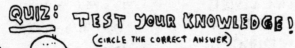

QUIZ: TEST YOUR KNOWLEDGE!
(CIRCLE THE CORRECT ANSWER)

YOU SHOULD NOT LET A HYDRO-CEPHALIC TRY ON YOUR:

A. SOCKS
B. BELT
C. HAT

YOU SHOULD NOT BOAST IN FRONT OF A PARAPLEGIC ABOUT:

A. CHILDREN (yours)
B. THE SENSATION IN YOUR GEN-TALS.
C. YOUR BANK AC-COUNT

YOU SHOULD NOT SING WHICH SONG TO A DOUBLE-ARM AMPUTEE:

A. GEORGIA
B. I'M A LITTLE TEAPOT
C. BLOWIN IN THE WIND

A VAMPIRE SEES A CHILD WHO HAS AIDS: THE VAMPIRE SHOULD NOT:

A. MAKE A SANDWICH FOR HIM.
B. READ THE TORAH TO HIM.
C. BITE HIM.

YOU SHOULD NOT ASK A PERSON WITH A TRACHEA-RESPIRATOR IF YOU CAN:

A. BORROW FIVE BUCKS
B. MEET HIS FAMILY
C. USE HIS AIR HOSE TO BLOW THE LOOSE HAIR OFF YOUR SHOULDERS

CHAPTER 11

6:30 A.M. and the sounds of church bells and retching just about knock me out of my bed, positioned near the front windows of my ground-floor apartment on Davis Street. It's the Wake-Up Call at the End of Time. DONG! DONG! DONG! DA DONG! Saint Mary's Cathedral, half a block away, is summoning the insomniac faithful of the whole city to early mass. While at the same time, BLEAGHHH! BLEAGHHH! BUH, BUH, BLEAGHHH! Johnny the wino is raising his stomach contents from the depths of intestinal hell. Today he's got his ass planted on the brick ledge of my windows, not eighteen inches from the bed. Not all that unusual. Some people wake up to birds. I wake up to winos.

I can see him through the curtains but he can't see me. Finished with his retching, he spies some geriatric cleaning lady on her way to the Holy Ghost. "WANNA DRINK, CUNT?" he bellows. Johnny is locally famous for his obscenities, always delivered at the top of his lungs. There are about a dozen bums and winos floating around between my apartment and the cathedral, but Johnny is outstanding. He's a psycho as well as a very late-stage alcoholic. He yells filth continually, even when there's no one around to be shocked. If he spots me watching him, he stops making sound, but his lips go on moving. When he thinks I'm out of earshot, he starts cursing out loud again.

I roll my bed up to the sitting position, thank God for another beautiful day, and do my morning meditation. Keeping the spiritual mood, I turn on the TV and check out Geraldo Rivera fearlessly investigating bisexual cardinals plus a man who plays meat for a living—some public-spirited topic. Thanks to cable I can enjoy Geraldo at the crack of dawn.

Finally Alex arrives. He's forgotten his key, as usual, and so pounds on the window, which is latched shut. I have to bludgeon the latch open with the back of my hand, trying not to break any bones in the process—I can't feel it after all. I slip Alex my key through the window; he spends five minutes trying to get it to work in the outer door. "Hi, Alex, are you stoned?"

His totally bald dome turns red with annoyance. "Of course I'm stoned!" he snaps.

"Nothing in the cupboard," Alex reports from the breakfast front. "Nothing in the refrigerator, either. There's only this." He shows me a box of prunes so old there's a curse written on the back in hieroglyphics. I've got doctor's orders to eat cereal with the texture of barbed wire to aid my bowels. Instead, Alex goes around the corner to McDonald's and comes back with a couple of Egg McMSG's. There's probably more fiber in the dollar bills he used to pay for them.

Now it's time for my daily range-of-motion exercises. Alex stretches my legs, runs them through the motions they would experience in a normal day if I weren't paralyzed. This keeps them limber, prevents the tendons from tightening up, tones the muscles somewhat, and in general readies them for that wonderful day when touching a picture of Elvis Presley will cure me spontaneously.

During the exercises I always sing, to the tune of Little Eva's "Do the Locomotion":

> *Everybody's talkin' 'bout the range of motion*
> *Come on Baby, do the range of motion*
> *(do the range of mo-tion!)*

Alex is usually off in a reverie of marijuana nightmares as he takes my legs through circus contortions. You can see the tombstones in his eyes. Then he helps me swing into the shower chair, and it's time for the bowel program. I can't get into the bathroom of my current apartment. The one good thing about the government housing was its wheelchair-accessible bathroom, complete with bar and roll-in shower. You could be a very clean mugging-and-robbery victim. Now I look on in envy as the cat prances into my bathroom to do his number while I must crap in the kitchen.

Alex gives me a suppository and as usual stands around daydreaming.

"Alex, I don't pay you to stand around with your thumb up your *own* ass!" After years off and on as my helper, he's used to that.

It's always annoying when visitors drop by during my bowel program. So I have Alex greet them at the door with the rubber glove on his hand. Only the most constipated come in. Once, after seeing a story on *60 Minutes* reporting the use of trained monkeys to aid quadriplegics, I told Alex, "Sorry, you've lost your job. There's a rhesus monkey standing out in the hall with a box of rubber gloves and a jar of Vaseline."

For my "shower," also in the kitchen, Alex spreads a tarp, and I sit next to the sink and douse myself. I probably should move to a more accessible place, but I like being downtown, and downtown ground-floor apartments are cramped. The alternative would probably be out in the suburbs, "The White-Trash Crest Apartments"—a defunct Jacuzzi as the main attraction, turds from small dogs all over the lawn, and a neighborhood social life revolving around the Minit Mart.

So I get all clean in my makeshift way and get toweled off, at which time Biggie, my nineteen-pound cat, jumps into my lap. Biggie sleeps in a cupboard twenty-two hours a day, rising only at bath time and at 2:00 A.M., when I am finally getting to sleep, to cover me and the bedspread with shed hair. Job done, the cat grants me a few kisses, walks around the house once, yowling and spraying, climbs back into the cupboard, and goes to sleep.

Once a week, just after my shower, we have to change the urine apparatus that is patch-glued to the permanent opening at the lower right-hand corner of my stomach. I slip back onto the bed. The old glue gets scraped off and a new self-adhesive patch, tube, and bag unit is pressed on. If it's not done just right, I leak. I've been writing a song about this:

> *I broke my neck upon a rock*
> *And now I cannot feel my cock:*
>
> *The doctors filled me up with fibs*
> *And now I piss between my ribs. . . .*

I can see Neil Diamond singing it.

During all of this the phone rings continually. My New York agent calling to make sure I'm going to deliver what he's promised. Editors, people working on the film projects, friends, relatives. . . . Deborah Levin, my manager, calls to make sure I'm not going to wimp out on her. She's where I get three quarters of my strength, a hard-driving, humorous woman, constantly kidding and prodding me. "Did you send that stuff for the licenser? Did you draw the 'Gag of the Week'? Did you do the photocopies for chapter nine? Did you get a haircut for the *People* magazine photograph? Did you put the cat out?"

"John, there's a guy on the phone says he's from the Sexually Transmitted Diseases clinic. He wants to ask you some questions." Kevin.

A few minutes later the phone rings again. "John, I've got some important news! Are you sitting down?"

Finally the moment comes for me to put my pants on crooked. My attendants have tried everything. We've called mathematicians, surveyors, Calvin Klein. . . . It's just as if the gods said, "Let there be one poor slob whose pants aren't straight one day in his life." I've considered having my nipples moved off-center surgically so that they will line up with the pants.

At last I'm in my chair, Walkman in my lap, cartoons to photocopy, mail or deliver wedged in by my thigh. This is the moment of freedom! It's noon, and I won't be meeting my attendant until nine. So it's good-bye to Alex and out the door for me.

It's noon recess at the parochial school across the street from the cathedral. The children are playing in Saint Mary's schoolyard. The sight of them gives me a chill. Boys dressed just as I was, twenty-five years ago, in salt-and-pepper cords, white shirts and blue sweaters, girls in white shirts and blue jumpers with pleated skirts. On the same block is the Hennessy, Brolin and McGee funeral parlor, through which Callahan corpses have been processed for generations. I remember when I was the age of these children, sitting still as death in the little parlor there, waiting for Grandpa Joe to twitch.

First thing today, I have a few errands to do in my own neighborhood, northwest Portland. In general it looks like downtown San Francisco but with more vegetation. There are handsome parks everywhere where you can be mugged and killed easily. A young man was found with his throat slit in the one three blocks from my house last weekend; the body was hanging in the children's play structure. The wallet was missing, but the expensive watch, a gold chain, and gold cufflinks were not taken.

First stop is Elias's Grocery, an old-fashioned neighborhood store with two items for sale: Thunderbird wine and chili weenies. Elias is Greek. His store caters to winos and serves as a social center for Elias's Greek cronies. I go there to cash checks. Elias has been cashing my checks for years, and he pretends it still annoys him. When I push the door open with my wheelchair, he says, "Ya gonna cash a check today, Yonnie?"

"Sure." I buy a bag of peanuts to mollify him.

"Hey, Yonnie, when ya gonna bring *60 Minutes* in here? You gonna cash a check on *60 Minutes,* Yonnie?"

After Elias's, I get some photocopying done, check the answering machine back at my apartment, then roll toward downtown on West Burnside, one of Portland's least fashionable but most characteristic streets. Once a wagon road, it now descends from the affluent West Hills to end among missions and warehouse buildings on the waterfront. There are a million street people out here, just a million! I love the street, the winos, the psychotics, the Christians . . . . I always run into about fifty people walking along with their hands outstretched, wild-eyed, their hair standing up like John Brown's.

I've forgotten my watch, but it's no use asking for the time in northwest Portland. You're likely to get answers like: "I think it's about noon." Someone else will overhear this and shout, "No no no, it's close to midnight!" A lot like my old haunts in Venice, California.

The beggars always hit on me, for some reason. Big, able-bodied geeks with fifths of wine in their hands ask, "Hey, buddy, got any money?" I say, "Look, haven't we got our roles reversed here? Shouldn't I be asking *you* for money?" Actually I feel a little out of place on Burnside because I haven't got a shopping cart filled with bottles and old clothes. With hundreds of wino-bagos on the street, the competition for refundable cans and bottles is intense. These are hard working street people. Throw a can in a dumpster and someone will catch it neatly before it hits bottom.

Whores also hit on me. Assuming I'm not getting any because I'm in a wheelchair, they sing out, "Hey, can I ride in your lap?" Usually I tell them I'm a Mormon. It works, unless they're Mormon themselves.

Things get more affluent as I approach the Galleria, a huge building with a covered atrium that has been converted into downtown's most fashionable shopping center. People with petitions prowl all over the place.

"Sir, would you like to sign a petition supporting the anti-obscenity bill?"

"Fuck no!"

Mixed in with the petition circulators are cute young girls hired to hand out cigarettes, get you hooked on the latest poison. I tell them no thanks, "My arms are paralyzed." Right in front of the entrance to all the mod shops stands the inevitable communist peddling *The Revolutionary Worker.*

Inside the Galleria, over my first cup of coffee, I enjoy the view. In the background are yuppie shops. In the foreground, using up all the tables at *La Pâtisserie,* sit a throng of thirteen-year-olds in black leather with half their heads shaved and the other half dyed bright orange, green, or electric blue. I sometimes wonder if they have problems with sex-starved parrots trying to mate with them. To think of all the energy I wasted, those many years ago, trying to get my father to let me grow my hair as long as John Lennon's. Dad was right all along, just three decades too soon. I can hear today's parents snarling, "When are you going to grow your hair out and get a job?"

Today I'm meeting Celeste, a friend who's an airline stewardess with PSA and in town for about sixteen minutes. I'm definitely falling for her: she's in her late twenties, a brunette with high cheekbones, full lips and big blue eyes. She has a short New Wave haircut and wears a beautifully tailored mauve authority-figure uniform that makes me want to fall down and grovel at her feet. "Hi, Numb Nuts!" she greets me. Celeste loves to give me a hard time.

When I had to get through three days of interviews for Maria Shriver's *Sunday Today* show on NBC, Celeste canceled her flights to nursemaid me through the whole exhausting thing. She just stayed in town and crashed on my couch. Today I pay her back with lunch at the Hilton, a block away, where PSA reserves rooms for its stewardesses. She holds my arm as I roll along and we laugh continuously. Celeste has a true gag sense, it's her best feature. But she looks fantastic, and I can't help telling her about it.

"Compliments, compliments, compliments! Do you want to have lunch or do a pork job on me?"

"I'll take the pork job. But if you want, we can eat lunch first."

Celeste is always bringing me things; today it's a sweater from Pittsburgh, a town she hates. She's from San Francisco, but really lives all over the continent. For me to get to a party in the suburbs takes a major effort; but Celeste hops on planes as if they were skateboards and routinely hits three major cities in a sixteen-hour day.

After lunch we zoom around town, Celeste hanging onto my arm. I buy her some knickknack she wants. I don't know what it is, but it falls under her label of "cute." Finally we stop in Waterfront Park under a gray, windy, forbidding sky. Celeste sits on the bench, I park beside her, and we're quiet for a while. Soon she'll go.

"What are you thinking about, Callahan? A gag?"

"Yeah. I'm working on an evolution gag."

"I'm gonna have to leave you to it." I take her back up the hill to the Hilton and the airport limo. We kiss. "So long for now, Numb Nuts."

On the way back to the Galleria, where I have an appointment with David Milholland, one of my editors, I stop repeatedly to say hi to the shopkeepers I know. I'm highly visible in Portland. I'm constantly being greeted, which I enjoy. As I roll along the sidewalk, a bus driver will roll down his window and yell, "Hey, Callahan! I loved the lawyer joke." Or Mayor Bud Clark will pedal up on his mountain bike. "You're John Callahan, aren't you? I loved the rectum joke!" But I enjoy it just as much when someone says, "Your work is sickening. You should be dropped from the paper!"

While I'm at the Galleria, I pick up some groceries at the health food store. I'm interested in avoiding too much sugar and preservatives, but nonetheless I'm amused by the health addicts in orthopedic sandals, muslin clothing, berets or fezzes, people

"My client objects to the endless delays in this trial. Attorney fees alone, he says, are becoming increasingly painful to bear."

who don't believe something's worth eating unless it comes from a bin. They are being suckered just like supermarket shoppers. And they don't seem to appreciate a sign that always cracks me up: "These eggs were laid by chickens that were hand-fed." Why not "These eggs were laid by chickens whose owners wore Birkenstocks"?

The conversations in the checkout line are dynamite. "Yes, groatbutter is so good for the intestines, and I always add some fish oil and purge my colon every three days. . . ."

"Well, *I* always have a certain amount of lecithin and muck-athin in my diet to cleanse my kidneys. . . ."

A special attraction of the health food store is a bulletin board on which the nutritionally advanced seek each other out. I always read it closely as it's a treasure house of ideas and information about our era: "Harmonious male, backpacker, into making sixteenth-century stringed instruments, seeks radical lesbian feminist household which will not tease me about my testicles."

David Milholland is the editor of *The Clinton Street Quarterly*, a showcase for new talent, distributed in San Francisco, Portland, and Seattle. It's in his paper that I've been able to develop the longer pieces that have become increasingly important to me, pieces such as "The Lighter Side of Being Paralyzed for Life" and "How to Relate to Handicapped People."

Besides being a tremendous editor, David is very funny himself and a great fan of comedy. He arranged a lunch for me to meet Graham Chapman of Monty Python, brought my work to the attention of Tom Robbins, and serves as my best critic, sounding board and *ex officio* psychologist. Today we've got the rough of a new piece about my dad spread out among the coffee cups on the Galleria table and, as usual, David is trying to reassure me that it will work.

"Yes, John, it will be a classic."

"But will it be a *major* classic?"

"Yes, John, it will be a major classic."

"But, David, I don't want to do it unless it's an absolute classic."

"It will be an absolute classic."

"But, will people think it's funny?"

David is also available for agonizing between six and nine each evening. I like that about him.

After my meeting with Milholland, I perform my most important daily task: I bring hot coffee down to the parking garage where my friend Kevin, a lost Irish poet, is to be found parking cars and nursing his hangover. I listen sympathetically to a fifteen- or twenty-minute account of how much it hurts, where it hurts, the pulsating nature of the pain, what the other symptoms are, how the hangover came to be, how much sleep he did not get, where he drank the night before, how much he drank, how much he plans to drink this very night, and would I mind getting him a couple of beers to help him over the rough part?

To obtain Kevin's couple of beers, I have to cross the street to the Yamhill Marketplace, more urban yuppification. Just enough of a fresh produce market has been left to anchor fifteen espresso stands, a fish market, a shoeshine, an exotic butcher (camel steaks, anyone?), a cheese shop, and a "Chicago-style" deli, all horribly overpriced. Shelly, of the deli, complains to me about my latest cartoon atrocity.

Before delivering Kevin's relief, I must empty my urine bag. I have to do this often because the bags are small. I'm grateful to discover, when I get to the men's room, that the wheelchair access stall is not occupied. Quite often there will be someone in there fighting heavy constipation in the only stall at the Marketplace

that I can fit into. So I sit there, listening to the painful gasping, and pray my bag doesn't spring a leak as I wait.

I'm an expert on downtown toilets. There are only twelve or fifteen accessible men's rooms in the city center. My plan is to team up with a woman quadriplegic and publish an illustrated guidebook, complete with maps, for the use of people in wheelchairs. We'll call it *Pissing Around Portland*.

Often I get trapped in the bathroom. Quite a few of the doors are easy to push open from the outside, but then I can't maneuver the chair to pull them open again from the inside. I try to empty my bag during high-traffic, full-bladder time periods, but that doesn't always work out. I've spent hours in one can in particular, up at Good Samaritan Hospital.

People ask, "What do you do? How do you fight down panic when you are stuck in the bathroom?" Anyone who walked in on me suddenly at such times might be startled to see me doing vigorous arm exercises, which I do when I'm bored. Or perhaps I'll be meditating or singing out loud. I jot down cartoon ideas, rewind my Walkman, do anything I can to keep at bay the dark prospect of being isolated and totally forgotten for a day, a night, a lifetime.

By the time someone opens the door, I'm so grateful, I almost fall out of my chair around his feet crying, "I've been so lonely!"

After bringing beer to the Lot Sot, as I call Kevin, it's time to visit my other local editors, drop off cartoons, pick up my mail. I'm still published at Portland State, so usually that's where I'll go first. It's on a tree-lined park, the girls are gorgeous, and there's always something going on. But I always feel self-conscious, too old around there. I half-expect a security guard to come and prod me with his nightstick. "Look, buddy, Do you think you could move out of the way? We got a lot of young people trying to get an education."

The land slopes downward from Portland State to the city center, and I really blast along. I usually have a wreck each day. I'll be flying down Broadway at the speed of light just as the offices empty out and thousands of young secretaries hit the street with their high heels clicking, everyone heading for a bus; suddenly I'll hear that old telltale clunk. The drive belt! Either I smash through a jewelry-shop window or into a small Chinese grandmother, fresh off the boat, whose first experience of America is to be pinned to the sidewalk by a one-hundred-eighty pound quad in a three-hundred-fifty-pound wheelchair.

In the middle of Portland is Pioneer Square, a brick-paved piazza surrounded by oddball architectural elements: headless columns, partial walls, a surrealist's idea of a civic space. When it was built a few years ago, it was briefly the in place for secretaries and young executives to bring a bag lunch. But it was quickly taken over by jive experts, dope pushers, and various other fringe elements, each of whom claimed their own territory. The whores and pimps have one corner; they don't mix with the bloods, whose ghetto blasters are tuned to Run DMC; in turn the bloods keep away from the white trash with *their* boom boxes set to Satan; everybody keeps his distance from the Mall Prophet. The Mall Prophet is a fifty-year-old toothless hippie with his hair in braids, wearing a woman's dressing gown, who reads palms and sells earrings he makes himself from IUDs. He's what remained of the Age of Aquarius when the acid wore off.

I stop at *Willamette Week* to drop off a new gag and pick up my letters for the day. "Dear Mr. Callahan," they usually begin, "How *dare* you be so offensive to (fill in oppressed minority)." The noble defenders.

Right across the street from *Willamette Week* is temptation: a topless bar. I decide not to go in. Due to my Catholic upbringing I can never bring myself to look upward in those joints. A girl would have to have her tits mounted on her knees for me to experience stimulation. Try as I may, I can never work up the nerve to look up and make eye contact. I'm positive the topless dancer would catch me looking and say, "Okay, Callahan, get your eyes down!"

Instead, errands finished, I retrieve Kevin and head for the Metro. The Metro is trendoid, a giant café in the European style, with sidewalk tables and featuring different cuisines of the world—French, Italian, Spanish, Greek—served from buffets around the interior. I always get lots of ideas from waiters. I have one gag showing a guy in a restaurant sitting on the floor, the waiter hovering over him with his pad and pencil. The customer is saying, "Well, today I think I'd like to start out with a chair, a table, a menu. . . ." Now, watching the clients bent over Hindustani eye of lamb or Nigerian cow belly *en croute,* I think of a variation.

CALLAHAN

" will that be all , sir ? "

Kevin returns to the table with a pitcher of beer and a glass. "Shit! I brought a glass." He launches into stories of how the Christian Brothers would smack him on the head when he was a kid. We trade school stories. It's like talking to a brother, and Kevin is the one friend who can really keep me in stitches. If I say, "Get me another drink, will you, Kevin?" He'll come right back with "Get it yourself, you crippled son of a bitch." But I get back at him. He is a total homophobe. Once I ran out of cash and had to write a check. I need both hands for that, and I asked him to steady the checkbook on my lap. There were at least fifteen beautiful girls standing in line, within earshot, at the buffets as I said, "And this time keep your hands off my genitals."

There's something in both of us that makes us revert to Catholic schoolboys when we're together. Kevin has a marvelous turn of wit that relates everything to a central *leitmotif:* his dick. If I ask him how he feels about the upcoming Mike Tyson fight, he'll say, "That man makes my dick vibrate with annoyance." If I ask,

"Kevin, isn't that a beautiful blonde there in the corner?" he'll answer, "John, when I see a woman like that, I have to take out my dick, stick it in a drawer, and then slam the drawer as hard as I can thirty-six times." Kevin disapproves of the upscale, West Hills girls I often date, preferring earthier, working-class types himself. "John likes women whose asses you could crack an egg on but with the brains of a skink fox."

I can roll home quickly in my chair, but Kevin can't keep up with his bladder full of beer. So he rides the bus, but hates it, because as soon as he's aboard, he's dead meat. I'm so childish. I'll wait till the doors are about to close and then yell something like, "Now, don't be afraid to buy some Preparation H!" And Kevin will get this helpless look on his face. He'll be thinking, God, be merciful. Don't let the crippled bastard say anything else. Just let the bus go. Just let me get home and pee without further humiliation.

I head home alone, full of thoughts of the images I've collected and what I'm going to do with them. There are maybe twenty blocks to travel on the way back to my northwest Portland neighborhood. I take the back streets, the factory areas, which are almost deserted by eight o'clock at night. There are no whores, no beggars with tin cups, no hustlers or dopers along these empty streets, where a few men are still at work in the silent warehouses and breweries. It's a place I find comforting and peaceful. This is a very old part of town, with buildings nearly as old as the city itself.

But between Fourteenth and Sixteenth streets, eight lanes of freeway, roaring with high-speed traffic, gouge through the city in a huge trench. I cross the freeway by way of a bridge, halfway across which I always get a horrible chill, one I can feel in my bones. This is the same freeway on which I cracked up and became a quad, one thousand miles to the south.

I get this feeling of terrible, impending doom, and I can't get across the bridge fast enough. I always feel as though something is going to push me over the edge and kill me, or that the bridge is going to collapse under me. I have to remind myself that when I'm across, I will be at the cathedral, a block from home.

Feeling like a hunted animal, I reach safety under the tall, Romanesque facade of Saint Mary's. It looms high above me in the night sky with its sculpted saints and the peaceful face of the Blessed Virgin above the ten broad doors. It is huge and self-contained, joined to the right of the facade by a walled court-yard to the convent of the teaching nuns and, beyond, the rectory, where the priests are just sitting down to their suppers after vespers. I stop here, even though it's windy and beginning to rain. The wind is moving the bell. I can hear the bell sounds, broken by the wind, and the rain is stinging my face.

The winos are crouching in the little shelters that the doors and buttresses of the church provide. I can just make them out. They are in their own niches, below the saints and martyrs.

An ancient beauty holds me here, and an old resentment keeps me at a distance. I try to live a spiritual life. Yet I feel damaged by the church.

Some of the winos call out for money. A few priests and nuns hurry in their hoods across the courtyard to some evening task.

People sometimes say, "You have such strength and you've been through such tragedy." And I always remember the cartoon I drew years ago of an obese man who has fallen flat on his face and spilled all of his candy. He's thinking, "What kind of a God would allow a thing like this to happen?" When I think of this cartoon, I realize I don't feel sorry for myself anymore.

I found something when I dropped the wine bottle ten years

ago, some kind of strength. Something I can depend on when my props have all been jerked from under me.

And I'm more surprised than anyone that I have adapted to this way of life. Sometimes I still wake in panic in the night when I discover I cannot move my legs, just as I did sixteen years ago on that night in L.A. And I panic again at the thought of having to spend the rest of my life in this condition. I wonder if I will survive it. It's true I've had to be a scrapper. I've had to work exceedingly hard to survive; before all else, it takes me three hours just to get ready in the morning.

But deep inside I know I'm always right where I'm supposed to be at the time. I don't want self-pity. I don't allow it. I want to grow. My life certainly has a black side but in other ways it's almost charmed. I always knew it would be. It's really satisfying in quite a wonderful way.

I feel I have a special calling. And when I do the work I was born to do, I get a sense of fulfillment that keeps me going. I see reasons for the things I've lived through. I don't have any remorse. And I can see the suffering of people around me now.

I'm getting soaked, it's time for me to go home. I enjoy getting home and seeing Marlos, my night attendant, with whom I speak French, my minor in college. Marlos speaks more languages than a possessed girl. He's Brazilian, a very quiet, generous-hearted person.

Marlos helps me get out of my wet clothes and into bed. I do my exercises, and he brings me a cup of tea. My cat jumps up into my lap, my nineteen-pound cat eager to make his nightly deposit of hair. Marlos and I chat.

Often a neighbor, Aloysius comes over. He's seventy-two, a saintly figure, the sexton of the cathedral. Or friends wander in, maybe Kevin, maybe my friend Michael Krupp, a comedian and the son of a comedian, Stanley Myron Handelman. Like me, Michael loves to twist the old, old gags: "I just rolled in from Vegas . . . my ribs are killing me!"

I'm comfortable in my bed, surrounded by my friends. It's nice and warm and we have a good time, but eventually even Kevin will decide it's time to go home. Every time he'll get up, notice he's too drunk to walk, and start fumbling with the phone.

"Relax, I already called the cab."

"Johnny, you're a fucking genius."

"That's why you're parking cars for a living and I'm on Welfare."

By eleven o'clock Marlos has left and I'm set up for the night with the thousands of papers I have to rewrite or edit or redraw. I'm working on three projects at once.

I may have been dragging a little. I may have been tired and depressed all day. But at night it's my time. I come alive. I roll my bed up, and I work with the TV on. I've got a remote to change the channels, and the light switches work by handclaps. There's a microwave at my elbow for hot drinks. My cat is curled up on the bed, and the streetlights throw quivering shadows across my drawn curtains.

I feel stimulated, magical. At night I seem to think more clearly. I work hard, but it doesn't feel like work to me. The intellectual clutter of the daytime hours dissolves from my mind, which moves almost in an instinctual, animal way. I'm happy. I don't care that the job—and the Welfare office—are giving me gray hairs or that I'm not rolling in dough, because ideas and images are flowing through me and out onto the paper.

Before the inspiration of this night fades into fatigue, I want to draw one more cartoon, one that started forming in my mind earlier today as I sat with Celeste at the river's edge. It's a variation of the old schoolbook cliché of the evolution of man.

The drawing shows a cutaway view of the sea meeting the land. In the sea you can see the primordial starfish; higher above, just climbing out of the water onto the beach is a lizardlike creature, half fish, half whatever. Higher still on the beach, completely out of the water you see a lemur; above him on the beach is a chimpanzee. He is followed by Neanderthal man and finally, at the highest point on the beach, before a podium, stands a twentieth-century *Homo sapiens,* dressed in a tuxedo and clutching a trophy. He's saying, "I'd like to thank all those who made it possible for me to be here tonight."

And then, I'm going to go to sleep.

CALLAHAN

"I'd like to thank all those who made it possible for me to be here tonight."

ACKNOWLEDGMENTS

My first and greatest thanks to Liza Dawson and Stacy Schiff of William Morrow and Company, Inc. In addition to being the most sensitive and intelligent of editors, I truly appreciate their not calling me a sexist pig and pushing me down the stairs.

Deborah Levin, my representative, dear friend, and surrogate mom, conceived this project and humiliated me until I got it done. Richard Pine, our agent, believed in it from the first and convinced everyone else, even me. David Milholland, himself a fine editor, read all the drafts, good and bad, made crucial suggestions, and was available for agonizing twenty-four hours a day. Thanks also to Gene and Norma, Jerry Fine, Larry Wobbrock, and my friends at Applause.

Finally, David Kelly, working from hundreds of hours of my tapes, drafted each chapter and then rewrote it again and again and again and *again* until no trace of his own voice remained. "We're not going to have one of those goddamn 'as-told-to' books," he would snarl. And we don't.

ABOUT THE AUTHOR

JOHN CALLAHAN (1951–2010) was a nationally syndicated cartoonist known for his frank portrayals of challenging subjects, in particular disability. Callahan, who became a quadriplegic following a car accident at age twenty-one, drew cartoons that touched upon addiction, ableism, and the absurd. He was the creator of the Nickelodeon cartoon *Pelswick*.